Love & The Art Of Saying NO
A Journey Out of Codependence, People-Pleasing, and Over-Commitment

By Amy Susanna Copeland, MABC

ISBN 978-1-54395-591-0

This book is dedicated to:

My mom, Lindy, who told me so & taught me well & stuck around to watch me learn it the hard way anyway.

My dad, Lindsey, & my husband, Jim for your unwavering patience, support, & healthy love.

Dana & Darci, for loving others into heaven & yourselves into the ground.

Kristina for longsuffering & steadfastness, & being the biggest cheerleader a gal could ask for.

My counselor Elise for your help, wisdom, & starring in this book.

Nate & Ashley at Hoyt Creative for your loyalty, generosity, inspiration, & creativity.

My Kickstarter backers, who took a chance & put your money where your mouth is, & made this book possible.

Table of Contents:

1

Counselor, Know Thyself!

I have always had a strange, unquenchable fascination with junky reality television, particularly documentaries about subjects like Hoarders, Super Morbid Obesity, Addiction, and Spoiled Kids or Adults Who Never Grew Up. I've never been all that ashamed of my odd taste in television, because I have always been an avid people-watcher, and these shows and documentaries give me a unique glimpse into the otherwise private minds and routines of people who live extreme and interesting lifestyles.

It has long been my belief that watching extreme examples of human diversity and disorder allows us the opportunity to learn something deeper and more subtle about how more "normal" people's brains or behavior might work. I feel like watching immature, shallow, carefully edited footage of excessive people in extreme situations gives a magnified glimpse into more common thought sequences. Essentially, you get to observe someone's "behavior highlight reel," which is deeply appealing to a counselor-type person such as myself.

My favorite part of shows like these is not actually as much the featured "star," the morbidly obese person or the addict. I'm actually most interested in the people surrounding those "stars," the friends, children, spouses, and parents. Unfortunately, this is where I have a different interest than the producers of such documentaries, because I want to see extensive interviews, even counseling sessions, with the family and friends who *continue*, for instance, to bring unbelievable quantities of unhealthy foods to their super morbidly obese loved one, even after that loved one has become immobilized and completely dependent upon them.

I think to myself, "Why don't they just take the opportunity to start cutting back on the food, at least until their loved one has gotten back to a place where they are able to get out of bed and cook their own coffin nails?" Or, "Why don't they kick out their adult child who hasn't paid rent in years and refuses to get a job?" "Why do they continue to support an addict who has stolen from and endangered them over and over and over?"

These are, to me, the most extreme examples of codependency, in which the Enabler directly enables despite clearly visible and life-threatening consequences of the User's addiction.
In less prime-time-worthy situations, the same behaviors show themselves in most people's lives in

smaller ways. Why do we keep spending time with/making plans with/talking to that one friend who makes us feel sucked dry every time we see them? Why do we promise ourselves time and time again that we will create more freedom in our schedule only to sign up for the next 5 things people ask us to do, whether we want to do them or not? Why do we keep answering when we see that name pop up on the caller ID that drops a rock in our stomach and makes us wonder "Oh great, what is it this time?" *Why is doing nothing all weekend such a mythically rare accomplishment?*

As for me, I have struggled for as long as I can remember with people-pleasing. I'm sure this was a significant contributor to my fascination with other people who, in my eyes, were failing to say no in much more clear and obviously damaging circumstances - if I could figure *them* out, maybe I could teach *myself* a better strategy ("Doctor, heal thyself!"). I always felt that if I could crack the code between Users and Enablers in such extreme scenarios, I would have a key to the universal relationship issue of codependence and enablement.

Why do people provide those they love with rope to hang themselves?

Why don't they just say no?

And, perhaps the biggest question of all, why do I think all these things are related? Are not codependence, people-pleasing, and over-commitment three separate issues?

As it turns out, they are all connected. At the root of people-pleasing, you find a warped understanding of love and how to express it, as well as a damaged concept of how to measure our own worth in relation to the world. At the root of codependence *and* the root of over-commitment, (spoiler!) you actually find people-pleasing, and in turn, that same warped understanding of love, how to express it, and a damaged approach to measuring our self-worth.

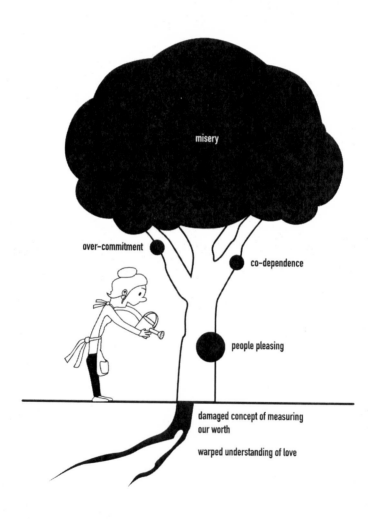

2

YES is a Habit

Before I pursued studying psychology, sociology, and finally counseling, I was a pastry chef for seven years. When I made the switch from my culinary career to being a full-time undergraduate student, I was determined to do it with as little debt as possible. I had a fair chunk of savings, which paid for about one year's tuition plus some living expenses, but I knew I would need to find a way to earn decent money while commuting over an hour to and from campus and taking 15 to 18 hours of class each semester. Because I wanted to give my studies a hundred percent of my attention, I couldn't handle a full-time job, and because I was in the latter half of my degree program, my schedule was at the mercy of the availability of my remaining required credits. This made even a part-time job, with a predictable schedule, a pipe dream.

So, I did what any broke, resourceful millennial would do. I posted statuses on Facebook, pleading for odd jobs. I offered everything from Christmas decorating, gift wrapping, and personal shopping to home organization, maid services, pet sitting, house sitting, private catering, and copy editing...- if you needed a job done, I would do it - for a price. I even found myself cleaning gutters, removing wallpaper in bathrooms, and on my hands and knees scrubbing and painting patios. Suffice it to say, my network came through for me big time, and through all the jobs my friends and family hired me to do, I was able to attend school, make ends meet, and work on the weekends and holidays without having to take on a "real" job.

Fast forward to my first year of married life and graduate school; my husband got a stable, if modestly-paying job, and I had a steady part-time job. That being said, by the middle of my third semester of Grad school, I was a frantic, anxious, and exhausted ball of stress. I had to take a step back. That was when I realized that all these extra commitments I had taken on were causing me so much unneeded stress. It wasn't my full-time graduate-level classes, or even the homework. It wasn't my steady job, which I did from home on my own schedule. It wasn't even my brand-new marriage and the new obligations that one might expect from that. It was the odd jobs. It was the many voluntary and paid commitments that I had never stopped making even though I was no longer single, broke, and unemployed. At that point, I had begun attending counseling as a requirement for my schooling, and my counselor pointed out that the things that were stressing me out the most were things I *didn't have to say "YES" to.*

I didn't *have* to say YES.

This was a completely foreign concept.

But, I did say yes. I realized I had gotten so deep into the habit of taking on any job that would pay while I was desperately in need of cash, that I hadn't ever taken a moment to assess my life and realize, "*Wait a minute! God has provided us with sufficient income to cover our needs, and even a few of our wants.*"

Our life may not have been luxurious, or even comfortable at times, but it was sufficient. If I had ever slowed down a moment and considered that I didn't have to say YES, I might have realized that one of the biggest reasons I always said yes to everyone *was no longer hanging over my head.*

So, the first lesson I learned about the habit of YES is that **I need to take a moment to reassess my priorities every time my circumstances change.**

I may not *need* to be a full-time student anymore now that I don't have Sallie Mae following me around, so, slowing down *is* an option that wasn't there before.

I may not *need* to budget the same for groceries, because my new school provides a food pantry for students to get necessities for free.

I may not *need* to clean that apartment, because my household income *is* sufficient to cover my necessities.

The next thing I learned is that **the habit of YES is, remarkably, as hard to break as any other habit.**

My friends and family were used to thinking of me first whenever any odd job needed doing or anyone was asking for recommendations. I didn't notice, until I realized I no longer *needed* to say yes, just how often I was given opportunities to do so.

What made it even harder, if I do say so myself, was the fact that I earned a reputation of providing a well executed service for a fair price. It made it easy to find work when I needed it, but it also gave me an unhealthy sense of pride in the fact that I felt I *needed* to say Yes. I felt that if I didn't say Yes, they wouldn't be able to find the same quality I could provide for the same low price, and it would somehow hurt them.

I made my clients' needs and/or budget my responsibility to such an extent *they* took precedence over my own time priorities such as school and relationships.

All of these Yes's nearly caused a serious breakdown. Even as I was discovering this side of myself in the middle of the semester, by finals I was still making cakes for a friend's wedding while being a bridesmaid, while attending all related functions, while attending a weekly family night across town, while volunteering four hours a week at church, while working a second job, "just for a month" for a friend's nonprofit, and I had just finished helping a hoarder clean out her apartment.

Enough was enough. I had to break the habit.

Practice Your Art

1. When is the last time you took a moment to step back, look at your life from a little distance, and reassess your priorities?

    _____

2. When is the last time your circumstances changed significantly?

    _____

    _____

3. If your answer to question 1 is prior to your answer to question 2, take this time to do so now.

    a. What are you saying Yes to?

        _____

        _____

        _____

        _____

        _____

        _____

    b. Why are you saying Yes to those things?

        _____

        _____

        _____

        _____

        _____

        _____

c. Have any of the circumstances
    surrounding your reasons for saying Yes
    changed since you started saying Yes to
    them?

_____

_____

_____

_____

d. Is it possible that the time has come to
    say No to one or more of those things? If
    so, what will your new No(s) be?

_____

_____

4. What have you said Yes to that you came to
    regret, or wish you had thought longer about
    before answering?

_____

_____

_____

5. What have you said Yes to this month?

_____

_____

6. There is a chart on the next page. In the first
    column, list a few of the big Yes's you've given
    in your life, and a few of the smaller more
    recent ones. In the second, write whether you
    were pleased with the choice you made to say
    yes, whether because of result or timing or

energy spent. In the third column, write your reasons for saying Yes to that commitment.

Commitment	Regrets? (Yes/No/Some)	Reasons

This exercise helps you learn to recognize when you have an option to say Yes or No, what motivates your choices, and how you prioritize your time and energy.

3

I Am as Responsible to Keep Promises to Myself as to Others

After the last chapter, you may be thinking, *"that's a nice autobiography, but I'm not in the habit of saying YES to paying jobs so much as to my friends, family, social commitments, and/or community service."* Don't worry! Breaking the habit of Yes is not specific to the types of activities you are overfilling your time with. It isn't even specific to time-sucks; you can say Yes to people taking your space and even your mental energy without committing a single minute to them.

Still, the solution is the same, and it's not simply "say NO."

When I reached a point of realizing that I had managed to overfill my life in spite of the fact that I had been aware of my habitual Yes-ing for months, my counselor and I talked about why being aware of a bad habit, while the first step, is not enough to break the habit.

I realized **I have a deep sense of responsibility**, which can be a significant strength, but it can also become a hindrance.

If I sense that someone is counting on me to help them, **I already feel committed before I even say Yes**, because I feel responsible to meet their expectation of me.

If I have committed to do something, I feel responsible to follow that commitment through to the end, even if the date moves from summer break to finals week, or the quantity asked is tripled, or I get sick.

BUT, my counselor pointed out, I never feel anything close to that sense of responsibility to keep promises to myself.

I couldn't argue. I had promised myself, I had even promised my husband, that I would cut back on my commitments, make time to focus on the most important priorities in my life, that I would cut back on my stress so that I could be happier and less frantic... every promise was broken. And every time I set those promises by the wayside so that I could say Yes to someone else, I convinced myself that I was the *only one* or the *best one* to do that job. Besides, once it was over with, I would have the rest of my life to rest, right?

Two huge problems were occurring. First, as a Christian, I was not trusting God to provide in the event that I was not available to say Yes. How full of it am I? God doesn't *depend* on me. Sure, He gives me, everyone, opportunities to serve on His behalf, usually so that we can learn something, but He does not *need* me to do anything. And what He *requires* me to do is love Him and everyone else. What I learned was that **I defined loving others as being available to help them**. I'll expand on what's wrong with that train of thought more throughout this book.

The second problem, I was not recognizing that **I am as responsible to keep promises to myself as to others!**

Self-care is vitally important in order to be able to effectively love others. When I over-committed myself by saying Yes, for example, to making a birthday cake for someone, I would then stress about finding or making the time to get the cake baked. I would feel like since I had offered a significantly more affordable price than any bakeries, I had obliged them to have me do the cake for them because it would be wasteful to pay for a cake somewhere else. This is a sort of convoluted train of thought, so bear with me, but if they felt like they had to select me to make the cake, I didn't want to put any limits on what they could ask for - after all, they couldn't choose another bakery, why should they have to change what they want just because *I* was making their cake?

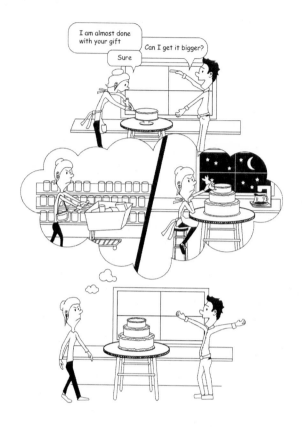

You can see how cyclical and convoluted my pattern could get. I was obliged to them because they were obliged to me until, ultimately, I was so stressed out and accommodating that I rarely turned a profit and even lost money. By the time I actually got to deliver the finished product I was so resentful of the whole endeavor (even though it was all my own fault!) that there was no joy and little love left in actually completing a task that was supposed to be an act of love and service.

When I make a choice to *self-care*, I take an opportunity to refill depleted love and energy reservoirs so that when I *do* pour into people, they are getting the best I have to offer, with sincere joy in blessing them.

Still, breaking a habit is never easy, and in my case, it took a cold-turkey approach to saying Yes. At the suggestion of my counselor, **I made a written, contractual promise to myself that I would not say Yes to any new responsibilities for 6 months**, and had my husband sign it as a witness.

As I wrote it I realized that it was a leap of faith; I was trusting that if I honored God in learning to make margin in my life, He would find *some* way to *manage* solving new problems without me. I know, it's ridiculous to read. But I had to really soak it in!

The second thing my counselor suggested was to **start a "No List"**, where I keep a log of every time I have honored my contract and said No when I could have said Yes.

I knew that eventually I would have to start balancing some Yes's with my No's, but this was an excellent habit-breaking exercise. I still feel a bit of victory every time I add something to my No List, because not only am I keeping my stress manageable, but I am remembering to trust God to handle things with or without my help.

Next, I learned that I need to treat all obligations like a business contract, even if money is not exchanged. I realized that a huge part of my over-commitment was the result of that feeling that once I had agreed to a task with one set of terms, I was committed regardless of

17

how vastly the terms surrounding it changed. In the business world, there is a term "Scope Creep[1]," (see Appendix) which refers to the unanticipated accumulation of small changes to an original project concept that ultimately results in significantly more time, effort, or extent of the final product than was accounted for in the original contract.

This *Scope Creep* is a huge factor for those dealing with problems with over-commitment. If it were a business contract, I would need to build a set, finite scope of change into the initial agreement before ever signing, and I would need to re-negotiate that contract every time those stipulations were exceeded. For example, take the cake scenario I outlined earlier. If I offered to a friend to make their wedding cake as a gift for a wedding in July, and then the wedding date gets pushed back to the weekend before all my finals are due in the following spring semester classes, that is a time for a whole new contract, or even dropping it altogether. And it is ok for me to cancel that offer. The entire ask has shifted.

When a friend asked me after I realized this contract idea to make her wedding cake, I told her right at the start that I would be honored, but I could only offer very specific options; limited number of flavors from a limited list of options, a maximum number of servings, size, number and types of fillings, etc. I wrote them all out for her and let her look over them to decide if what I could offer her without stretching myself too thin was a match for what she wanted. And then when, inevitably, new ideas came up and new flavors were wanted, I reinforced the original contract and explained that I would have to charge extra for additional flavors and fillings.

This approach worked in both parties' favors, and I felt genuinely excited to deliver the final product. This, like so much of the advice you will find in this book, seems so obvious when you are reading it, but it is so difficult for people-pleasers to actually learn to apply to their own lives. It will be your saving grace, though, and will save you grief and headache in the long run, allowing you to avoid burnout and please a lot more people in the end, *including yourself.*

Even if you do not have a formal written contract, every commitment is at least a verbal contract. If you can take the time *before* committing to write out a little contract for yourself, even if you never show it to the other party and make it official, you will better alleviate your own guilt or chagrin when that *Scope Creep* starts wiggling its way in to encroach on your best intentions, and it comes time for you to renegotiate the terms of your commitment.

Practice Your Art

1. What type of task or commitment do you struggle to say No to the most?

   _____

   _____

2. Who do you struggle to say No to the most?

   _____

   _____

3. What (if any) difficulties have you encountered as a result of people-pleasing or over-committing?

   _____

   _____

   _____

   _____

4. What would a self-care contract with yourself look like?

   "Dear _____, I promise _____

   _____

   _____

   Signed, _____ "

   • What promises to yourself have you broken?

   _____

   _____

21

5. Challenge yourself: start a short NO list just for practice below; record the next five things you turn down:

- _____

- _____

- _____

- _____

- _____

6. Follow up: Would you have ordinarily said Yes to any of the above listed things?

_____

7. Was it a struggle to say any of these No's? What made it hard? What made it easier?

_____

_____

_____

8. Think about the things you commit your time to that you feel can get out of your control. List a few below.

_____

_____

9. Choose one of the above-listed items and think about it as you fill in the "contract" template provided below: (An example is provided on the following page for ideas)

"I will commit to ____[task]_____ with ____[length of time]____ advance notice. I am only committing to ____[specific quantity of work, amount of time, quantity of materials, other unit of measuring the scope of your task]____. Additional ____[work, effort, time, materials]___ are outside the scope of this commitment and ____(circle one: [are not available] [require renegotiation of the contract and additional consent])____. I reserve the right to say No to requests outside the scope of this commitment.
This commitment will be fulfilled by ____[date/time frame]___ for ____[price if applicable]___.

(Optional:) Changes to commitment outlined above are limited to ____[List reasonable adjustments you are comfortable accommodating]____.

_____[Your Signature]_____
_____[Their Signature]_____ (Optional)

23

Example:

"I will commit to ___*Picking up from school, babysitting, and providing dinner for my nephew*___ with ___*at least a week's*___ advance notice. I am only committing to ___*Tuesday afternoons until 7:30pm during the spring semester*___. Additional ___*Babysitting requests*___ are outside the scope of this commitment and ___*require renegotiation of this contract or separate consent for singular situations*___. I reserve the right to say No to requests outside the scope of this commitment.

This commitment will be fulfilled by ___*Beginning of Spring Semester thru termination of Spring Semester, 1/5-5/20*___ for ___*Cost of gas, activities, occasional refills of nephew's favorite snacks, & a mug that says "World's Best Aunt"*___.

(Optional:) Changes to commitment outlined above are limited to ___*up to 1 of nephew's friends can join with at least 8 hours' notice, excluding the one who likes to break my appliances and make nephew cry on purpose*___.

_____*Amy S Copeland*_____

_____*Hypothetical Sibling*_____ (Optional)

24

4

People Pleasing Can Cause More Problems Than You Think

There is an obvious problem caused by People Pleasing: People Pleasers can become overwhelmed with responsibilities to live up to the expressed expectations of others. This means we struggle to say "No", as discussed previously, when people ask us to do things for them or even just make it clear they have a problem we are capable of solving.

But I realized in therapy that there were several issues in my life that were the result of a people-pleasing mentality, and I didn't have a clue they were linked to it. I had become bogged down with a sense of responsibility for EVERYONE's thoughts about ANYTHING I did. Here are some examples of how my people pleasing affected my life in unexpected ways:

First, I felt anxious about living up to the expectations of not only my parents, but of *everyone* who had *any* peripheral expectations about me. After I quit my first career as a chef to go back to school for counseling, I regularly ran into people from church who didn't even know me well enough to tell me apart from my sisters, but had once changed my diapers and therefore had genuine interest in what I was doing with my life. I felt responsible to go into a quick but thorough explanation and justification of all the factors that had gone into my decision, so that they wouldn't think of me as a flake, or a quitter, or worry about what I was up to now.

I felt like I had to explain the ministry I wanted to get into, not so that I could share the burden of my calling with them and share with them in prayer, but so that they would not get that look on their face that I saw so often when they realized that I'd left what they thought was a glamorous career for something more... common. I'm not sure to what extent you can relate to this, but I seriously felt exhausted at the thought of "catching up" with people, because I'm already absolutely terrible at small talk, and this need to explain my professional and personal decisions to everyone who asked was stressful.

Similar to the above problem was a pressure I felt to have a "simplified identity." This may be because I had identified with the simple-to-state and well-known identity of Chef for so many years, but I felt like I needed to have a single-sentence explanation of myself that was broad enough to help people feel like they knew something significant about me. I was prideful about calling myself simply a "student," because at my age I worried that people would perceive me as a career student, putting off real life by perpetually taking on classes and loans. Even now I catch myself telling new acquaintances "well, I *used* to be a Chef but now I'm...," as if what I do now isn't interesting enough to stand on its own. All of this was people-pleasing pride. Why should I care whether someone jumps to a wrong conclusion about me because they only know one thing about me?

Finally, I found that the anxiety I had been battling for about 4 years (which initially drove me to counseling) was a result of people pleasing! I was constantly anxious about facing potential failures or tasks I thought I might not do correctly. This was not because I thought I would die if I failed; it wasn't even because I worried about what would happen to my life or career if I *did* fail. I feared (I still fear) failure because I am terrified to disappoint those who are cheering for me. I don't want them to be wrong about me, I don't want them to be sad for me, I don't want them to feel stupid for believing in me, and I don't want to have to go through the embarrassment of *telling* them I've failed.

I could handle experiencing failure. What I couldn't handle, I realized, was being *seen* as a failure.

Here's the deal. If God came to me in an undeniable way and told me to, ohhh, I don't know, "sell everything I have, give the proceeds to repair wells in South Sudan[*], and live financially 'by faith,'" that would not actually be received well, even by Christians.

[*] Check out Water Is Basic at waterisbasic.org if you are interested in an awesome water charity that brings clean water to South Sudan

At best it might seem like an extreme, impassioned reaction to a scripture which many people interpret differently. At worst, it might seem like a cop-out, an excuse to quit and escape the responsibilities of life.

Even when it's scripturally sound, let's be honest with ourselves: People have an instinct to judge and/or diminish those things that make them feel convicted about their own choices, and it can make them inclined to be critical.

This isn't a diatribe about how people *should* react to others' life decisions. It isn't *bad* to give an honest, heartfelt opinion or bit of advice. But the point is that ultimately, **I need to only be concerned with what *God* wants me to do.** In fact, His way is *rarely* popular. I have a responsibility to confirm that what I believe to be His word in my life is in line with the Bible, and even to seek counsel and accountability with trusted biblical scholars, so that I can uncover those times when I am misunderstanding. But **it is not my responsibility to make sure every individual in the general public approves of my choices in life.** Sure, it's polite to give updates to people who are interested in your life, but I don't *owe* them that!

And it isn't my responsibility to protect them from the possibility that life is hard for me at a given time.

We are so trained not to burden people, to smile and say "I'm fine." That is the most rampant form of people pleasing for this Social Media generation. We learn to only post about our victories, or at most a somewhat humorous meme that provides a light-hearted reference to the things we struggle with.

It isn't just vanity. Ok, *sometimes* it is, but often it's a product of people pleasing that we don't dare be vulnerable on these forums. How many of you have seen a crack in someone's Facebook armor, where they dared to say "I'm struggling", and you thought, "wow, me too - I thought I was alone in that"?

Who are we protecting when we try to sugar-coat what we share with people for their sake?

It leaves us alone in our struggles, and it leaves them without opportunity to help us, feeling equally isolated in their own struggles.

Personally, I am still working on how to move past the effect that my concern for others' opinions has on my choices and behavior. What I'm learning, though, is how many problems in my life are sprouting from people pleasing. Learning to disregard other people's opinions is an ongoing effort. On the bright side, as they say, acknowledging the problem is the first step.

Practice Your Art

1. What are areas of life in which you worry about how others perceive you?

_____

_____

2. Where does that worry come from?

   - Are you avoiding criticism?

   - Are you afraid to disappoint someone?

   - Is it fear of embarrassment, or loss of status?

   - Is it necessary to keep a certain level of appearance appropriate for a specific setting, such as a highly professional work place, to which you have chosen to submit yourself?

_____

_____

3. Reflect on the list above. Are your fears well founded?

_____

   - Weigh: What, truthfully, is at stake if you fail?

_____

_____

4. If what is at stake is the regard, esteem, pride, or disappointment of others, what has it meant to your life so far to allow this to impact your choices and behavior?

_____

_____

5. What would it change if you freed yourself from this fear?

_____

_____

6. Reflection:

Take some time to reflect on those things in your life that seem to bring you stress. Consider whether they are worth the reward - some of them will be! The esteem of your employer may well be worth maintaining. But if there are any that aren't worth what you are giving up of yourself, start being aware of those things.

Begin to be watchful, as you live your life and move through this book, for the things you do and the choices you make, and *for whom* or *why* you do them.

This is a time for self-awareness and intentionality. Become a student of your own motivations, and consider tracking what you learn in a journal. I cannot tell you what you will find, but it is a universally beneficial practice.

_____

_____

_____

5

God's Calling Vs. The Approval of Others

I mentioned my struggle as a Christian to own and have confidence in the choices I've made based on the calling I believe God has for me when I try to explain it to some of the people who want to catch up with what's going on in my life. I came to realize that my anxiety was all about being hung up on what other people think about my actions, my choices, and whether or not they will approve.

So the simple thing I learned was that I can't be a people pleaser *and* be happy because sometimes God's calling is at odds with what other people think is best - even well-meaning people.

A few years ago, I got a strong urge to mix things up, meet my neighbors, and create a little fun in my community because I wasn't finding anything interesting to do, and my philosophy is if you want something and nobody else is providing it, you better do it yourself. So I decided to start throwing "Spontaneous S'mores Parties." I would get the stuff for making s'mores at the park, throw an announcement up on social media and text as many people as I could about an hour before it started, and then head to the park. I had to cajole my sisters and parents into coming with me to the first one, because I planned on sharing the s'mores with anyone who walked by and wanted one, and I figured a lone person standing next to a grill in the middle of the park would be a bit... off-putting.

My mom thought I was crazy. She might not have been entirely wrong, but it was clear she expected me to be a bit disappointed when the whole endeavor was a bust. Still, my family is nothing if not reliable. We all headed to the park, my little sister (about 15 at the time) sat down and started doodling with sidewalk chalk while we got the fire going, and I taped a big poster board that said "Free S'Mores!" onto the picnic table facing the sidewalks. People walking in the park started tentatively approaching the table. A few friends who had no plans that night showed up. Sidewalk chalk murals grew in every direction. A little family out for an evening stroll came, and the grandmother chatted with my mom while she roasted her marshmallow - she was leaving to move back to India the next day after living here for years and years. She had never had a s'more. What a perfect way to spend her last evening in America!

My mom told me later that she was glad I didn't let her doubts stop me. And now, sometimes when I have a hare-brained idea that my mom doesn't understand, she reminds herself of the s'more party and takes a leap of faith. That's why she let me drag her to an outdoor bar called the "Truck Yard" to find a caterer for my wedding.

Sometimes, we have "weird" ideas. Sometimes we see things from a unique perspective. **Sometimes that's God using us as the perfect tool for one perfect purpose that no one else's brain is the right shape to fit**. Just because people don't understand what you're doing, or they don't believe it's worth the risk, doesn't mean you shouldn't do it.

Sometimes people who are genuinely looking to protect you are too biased to get out of God's way, and you need to be firm, all by yourself, in your convictions.

When I was 15 or 16, I felt a strong inclination to join a mission trip my church was planning to Bogota, Colombia. My dad, an amazing man of faith, was not keen on the idea of his teenage daughter going with a group to one of the drug capitals of the world for a week to live in an orphanage and spend time in the slums with the street kids. I can't blame him for that! But I was resolute.

I made a deal with him. I was unemployed, so if God wanted me to go to Bogota, He would have to provide the money for me to go - my dad wouldn't have to pay anything. If I couldn't get the money together, I wouldn't argue and I wouldn't go. As the deadline approached, I had raised a remarkable amount of money through fundraising and odd jobs, but I was still a few hundred dollars short. Then I got word that a man - not a church member - walked into the church office and gave a check to the receptionist, telling her to "put it toward missions." It was just enough to cover my remaining balance for the trip. So I went! God did some incredible things during that trip, and I got home safely.

We all know Jesus was never particularly concerned with people pleasing, but He also found Himself called to do what was unpopular with those who loved Him. Toward the end of his ministry, Jesus was determined to go to Jerusalem even though it was dangerous to do so. He understood the danger and told his friends. His close friend Peter questioned him and tried to talk him out of going, but Jesus had strong words for him: "Get behind me, Satan! You are a hindrance to me. For you are not setting your mind on the things of God, but on the things of man."[2]

I mean, it goes without saying, Jesus did not lack for confidence in His calling.

Another awesome story of someone defying the "approved," "safe" opinion in favor of God's calling is that of Ananias in Damascus.[3] Ananias was sent by God to seek out a state-endorsed persecutor named Saul. He took the calling seriously and went, despite the danger.

Even dreams can be so easily shot down by people who think they're just helping regulate your expectations so that you aren't disappointed later. My husband and I have a plan and a dream to never take on debt if we can possibly help it. This includes a mortgage. We have our plan in place, but it is amazing how many well-intentioned people scoff or *kindly inform* us that such a plan is impossible, perhaps even irresponsible!

I'm not going to go into a whole sideline about my personal opinions on debt and its so-called necessity, but I'm still working on not letting people's disapproval of our dreams get to me.

The fact is, **dreams don't require the approval of others to be achievable**.

And for me as a Christian, if it's God's calling, who cares what they think?

Practice Your Art

1. Are you currently living out your dreams?

   _____

2. Do you have dreams for your future? Do you allow yourself to dream? (Yes/No)

   - If not, why not?

     _____

     _____

   - If so, are you pursuing them?

     _____

   - If not, why not? What is holding you back?

     _____

     _____

     _____

3. Write out any dreams that have fallen by the wayside as you have moved through your life:

   _____

   _____

   _____

   _____

   _____

   _____

   _____

   _____

4. Write out a few of your dreams for your future:

_____

_____

_____

_____

_____

_____

_____

5. What stands between you and these dreams?

_____

_____

_____

_____

6. What are you going to do about it?

_____

_____

_____

_____

_____

6

A Reason Is Not an Excuse

Entering counseling, I couldn't understand why I couldn't seem to avoid toxic interactions in my relationships. Why, no matter how hard I tried to communicate with my friends, they continued to take advantage of me - even when I knew they were *trying* to be better friends - and why I seem to attract those sorts of relationships in the first place.

My counselor had already been privy to the details of a few of my more toxic relationships, and she asked me to give examples of toxic friendships, and what my thought process was when one of them did something inconsiderate or took advantage of me. I described several friends who were sweet, who I knew desired to be good friends, but who only ever called me when I could do something for them. The friends would disappear when things were going well. They would only even answer calls, much less initiate them, if there was something I could do for them, whether it was to give advice, provide a ride to the dentist, or help them hunt for a job. I often vowed not to answer the next time they called, or to say *No* until I had some evidence that the friend had any inclination to make our relationship a two-way one. But the next time I saw them, or the next time they asked me for something, I would cave to (varied) friends like this because:

"They were never taught better by their parents. **I need to be an example of good friendship so that they can have a chance to learn how a healthy person behaves.**"

"They have been hurt repeatedly by previous friends, and they don't trust people. **I need to prove to them that there are trustworthy people in this world.**"

"They were mean to me because they were having a bad day. **It's not me they're mad at.**"

"They have clinical depression, so I need to be understanding and accommodate every time they are being selfish or rude because that's just a symptom of their illness. **They don't *mean* to be inconsiderate, even if this *is* literally the 10th time they've stood me up without calling.**"

"They've had an unfairly hard life, and this behavior is how they have learned to survive. **I need to be patient and model better coping skills.**"

I had also explained to my counselor on several occasions that I don't believe in "true" villains, which is to say that I don't believe people are evil on purpose

41

just because they're born with black hearts. Rather I believe they are hurting or angry or both, and reacting to whatever injustice they perceive has been carried out against them.

My counselor pointed out that **I was looking for** *reasons,* **and** *excusing* **people for those reasons.**

We all know that a reason is not an excuse, thanks to two kinds of experiences.

First, most of us have been in a place where we were late for something. When we saw the person we were meeting, we started to explain the legitimately outside-our-control circumstances that led to our tardiness, only to have the person say "I don't want to hear your excuses."

How utterly frustrating is that moment? We were just wanting to explain what happened, not asking to be excused because of it.

The second way we all know the difference between a reason and an excuse, is that there is a reason for almost everything a person does, and not all of those actions are excusable. For instance, "I just really wanted to," or "I didn't feel like it" are rarely excusable, but they *are* reasons.

Through a LOT of help from my long-suffering counselor, I came to realize that **just because there is a** *reason* **a person behaves badly, doesn't mean they are excused from consequences.**

Just because there is a *good reason* for a person's bad behavior, doesn't mean they are excused from being responsible for their actions.

If a child was raised by parents who took pleasure in violence, and was forced, encouraged, and rewarded by his parents to participate in animal mutilations, etc., and then that child grew up to be arrested for torturing dogs, we could understand that there was a *reason* for his behavior, but that doesn't *excuse* him from the consequences of his actions, in this case going to jail.

If a person has hypoglycemia, and it's been 6 hours since they last ate something, and it was a small salad, that is a valid *reason* for that person to be cranky. But it does not *excuse* them from their responsibility to not snap at the next person who asks them a question, just because they are hungry.

If a student is required to take an economics class as part of his degree program, and it is being taught by the most dull professor since *Ferris Bueller's Day Off*, and the class is at 7am, and the student DOES NOT CARE ABOUT ECONOMICS HE IS AN *ARTIST*, for heaven's sake! ... These are all *reasons* for that student to struggle in class, but none of these reasons *excuse* the student from receiving an F for sleeping through every lecture.

Are you pickin' up what I'm puttin' down?

Because when my counselor pointed this logic out, it was EMBARRASSINGLY NOVEL to me.

Understanding the reasons behind people's behavior can definitely help take some of the confusion and even the sting out of the hurts they inflict on us. It can help us have empathy. **But the *reasons* do not excuse the hurt**.

If my sister mistakes me for a burglar one night and hits me over the head with a skillet, she didn't *mean* to hit me, there is a *reason* she attacked me that has nothing to do with me, but the reality is that *my head still hurts*.

Just because he was abused as a child and learned to manipulate people to survive that trauma, doesn't mean his manipulation doesn't hurt his girlfriend.

Her hurt isn't nullified by his reasons.

Her hurt isn't *healed* by the fact that she understands *why* he does it.

A reason does not excuse a person from taking responsibility for their actions.

And I need to let people be responsible for themselves.

(And I need to be aware of when I should take responsibility for hurting others, even when I have a *really good reason* for my actions.)

Practice Your Art

1. Can you think of an example from your own life when a person has had *reasons* and expected to be *excused?*

   _____

   _____

   _____

2. Think of the people you struggle the most to have healthy boundaries with.

   _____

   _____

   _____

3. What are some excuses you have given to yourself for why you struggle to enforce boundaries with the people listed above?

   _____

   _____

   _____

   _____

   _____

   _____

   _____

   _____

7

When You Are Angry, Look for the Hurt

Understanding the source of anger may not appear on its face to be related to *The Art of Saying No*, but as you will come to see, recognizing anger and hurt, and understanding true forgiveness are vital to setting good boundaries in your relationships. Knowing *why* you say No when you say it is an art, too.

When you are angry, look for the hurt. This lesson is two-fold. I don't know which you'll guess first, but prior to therapy, I had learned to look for the hurt behind the attack when I felt angry or attacked. When someone was inconsiderate or hurtful to me, I remembered that "hurt comes from hurt" and I would rationalize why that person might be attacking. Had I injured them first, causing them to lash out in defense? Had they never been taught better because they were surrounded by people who were hurtful all their lives?

All of these are *reasons*, though, and in the last chapter we learned what is flawed about this pattern of thought.

The second, new interpretation of the concept of "When you are angry, look for the hurt" is that **when I am angry, I need to slow down and realize that all my own anger stems from a hurt**. I can be so blinded by my anger at a person that I never move past it. I think I forgive, but I really just decide I should probably not be angry anymore, and I stifle my anger towards that person until the next time they injure me, and **then I am twice as angry as before**. But if I can remember the principle that anger stems from hurt, I can begin to rationally tackle what hurt I am protecting with my anger.

What vulnerability did the person expose that made me defensive? What injury did they inflict that makes me feel imposed upon?

True forgiveness can't happen if I don't identify

That I am hurt
How I am hurt

True healing can't happen if I don't acknowledge that I'm injured.

A remarkable effect of looking for the hurt is that when you find it, the whole scope of the situation shifts. You aren't as angry because your faculties are occupied tending to your wounds. This separation from your anger allows you to have a more reasonable perspective on whatever you were angry about. Are you angry because the person caused hurt, but that hurt was the result of a true accident? It is easier to see this if you are willing to acknowledge the injury and not let your anger steer the ship.

Is this hurt pretty minor but the tenth or twelfth injury of its kind? That might explain a seemingly unreasonable level of anger at a relatively minor hurt.

Is this hurt familiar because someone else has hurt you in the same way? Another reason you might have an apparent overreaction.

This shift allows you to work on healing, on letting God heal you. This gives you time to work on forgiveness, grace, and practicing wisdom to identify possible changes in your relationship with the person who hurt you.

1. Flip back to this section at the end of chapter 6 and review your answers. Are there any feelings you have not allowed yourself to acknowledge or express as a result of those excuses?

   _____

   _____

   _____

2. Do you feel safe or free to experience negative emotions without worrying that they are not valid or they are in some way not fair to those who inspire them?

   _____

   _____

   - Do you understand your hurt is valid, and you are allowed to feel it, even if the person who hurts you does not acknowledge the injury or believe their actions were hurtful?

     _____

     _____

     _____

3. Reflection:

This is a difficult reflection, and entirely optional, but if this set of questions is resonating with you, you may need to learn how to give yourself space to be a human who has feelings and experiences hurt. You can also come back to this after moving on to the rest of the book. Schedule and set aside several hours for private reflection and self-care. Review the list below before you start, as you may need to prepare some materials ahead of time. If you have a history of trauma, self-harm, or drug/alcohol addiction, do not participate in this exercise without talking to a therapist, counselor, or sponsor first. It can be an intense and potentially triggering exercise. Start by journaling:

- List those who are otherwise close to you around whom you do not feel safe expressing genuine emotions.

- Consider what specific examples made you think of these individuals.

- Write out the hurts you do not feel safe acknowledging to them, or possibly to anyone.

- Allow yourself to acknowledge those hurts, the anger, etc. It may seem like a strange thing, but give yourself room to *feel*, to cry, yell into your pillow, throw ice at a brick wall (the impact and shatter can be very satisfying if your emotion is frustration or anger), or even just sulk for a bit.

- Put a time limit on it. Make it reasonable, give yourself enough time to visit that part of yourself and process, and then come out of it and care for yourself before you have to run and pick up your kids or go to work, but put a cap on it.

- Now, comfort yourself. It should go without saying, but avoid alcohol and drugs during this exercise. You are creating a tool kit for safe coping. Treat yourself to a favorite snack or warm beverage. Watch a feel-good movie. Call your spouse or a friend who you trust to let you experience genuine emotions safely, and let them know you could use some cheering up. Go for a walk. Do a craft. Write a poem. Visit a trampoline or rock-climbing park. Look at Christmas lights. Go to the pet store and hold a bunny. Go swimming. Listen to your favorite album while taking a relaxing bath. Drive on an empty highway with the windows down & the music loud. Begin to teach yourself to both experience your feelings, and cope with them in healthy ways.

- If you find that through this exercise you feel as though you have broken down a dam that was holding back an overwhelming amount of emotions that are difficult to navigate, this is a strong sign you need to see a counselor or join a support group until it is reduced to a manageable level, and you are equipped to manage it on your own. Be encouraged; you *can* get to that point! But don't be afraid to seek help in the meantime.

8

Forgiveness Is for the Forgiver

Forgiveness. This has been a theme throughout my journey out of codependency and people pleasing. I have begun to hypothesize that most people on this journey need to work with forgiveness at some point, because one thing everyone on the planet over the age of 2 has in common is that we have all suffered injury from of another person, and we all need to learn to understand the act of forgiveness.

Possibly the most important thing I have learned about forgiveness is that it is *for the forgiver.* Many people look at the act of forgiveness and they see a benevolent gift of forgiveness being extended to the wrongdoer. It is in the category of actions that make a person the "bigger person," an entirely optional choice that the injured party has the power to withhold or distribute at his exclusive discretion. This perspective on forgiveness makes the idea that forgiveness is for the *forgiven* a common and believable myth.

However, when you think about it backwards, **unforgiveness is most injurious to the person in a position to extend it.** Forgiveness is an opportunity to take your hurt, look it in the face, and hand it over to God to heal. True forgiveness allows you to overcome your hurts in such a way that it can even appear to onlookers as transcendent. This may seem like awfully dramatic language, but give me a better word for the look of peace on the face of a woman who has forgiven her child's murderer.

Sure, there is a healing that can be experienced by the forgiven, but that benefit is almost incidental, because how often does forgiveness need to happen when the forgiven will never know, or does not seem to care, or does not believe they have done anything that would require forgiveness?

A rape victim may never know the name of the person he or she needs to forgive. An abusive parent may pass away before his or her victim comes to a point where they are able to forgive them. Possibly the hardest scenario is when a person is alive, identified, and seen regularly, and they have no remorse whatsoever. In such cases, forgiveness is 100% for the forgiver, and **it is vital to avoid becoming bitter.**

The fact is, a person is capable of inflicting injury without any intention of doing so, or any understanding of why. They may have inadvertently reopened a wound neither of you even knew you had, and it may really be a situation where they hurt you but they did not knowingly do anything "wrong." In such cases, while a good friend might still apologize for hurting you, ultimately it is between you, your hurt, and God (and maybe your counselor) to work through forgiving that injury, and then work on identifying the *original* injury and forgiving *that*.

PLEASE realize that forgiveness is vital to avoid becoming bitter. **Bitterness is paralyzing to the heart.** It attracts cynicism, lack of trust, callousness, and an inability to let love, joy, and peace in. In fact, when you think about it, every one of the fruits of the Holy Spirit listed in Galatians 5:22-23, (Love, Joy, Peace, Patience, Kindness, Goodness, Faithfulness, Gentleness, and Self Control) are weakened, if not prevented altogether, by bitterness.

Practice Your Art

1. Is there anyone you are struggling to forgive in your life?

_____

_____

2. How is it impacting you?

_____

_____

_____

_____

3. What is making it difficult for you to forgive them?

- Are they continuing the offending behavior, re-inflicting the injury?

- Are they unapologetic?

- Are they not around anymore?

- If none of the above, write your answer here:

_____

_____

_____

4. Is there anything you fear at the thought of forgiving a certain person?

_____

_____

- Where do you think that fear comes from?

    - Are you worried you will open yourself up to re-injury by the same person?

    - Are you concerned you will open yourself up to similar injury by someone else?

    - Are you concerned the person will not realize the scope of their offense?

_____

_____

_____

_____

_____

_____

_____

_____

_____

9

What Forgiveness Is NOT

How do you *know* whether you've truly forgiven someone? How do you know the process has worked?

It is common for people to believe that you haven't truly, completely forgiven someone until you are willing to let them back into your life, perhaps even until you have returned to the same degree of relationship you had before they offended you. I find that this opinion is most popular among those who are the offenders looking for their life to return to normal.

However, **forgiveness is not evidenced by reconciliation**.

There are several reasons this is true. First, as discussed in the previous chapter, there are many circumstances in which a person must forgive someone who is not remorseful. In these cases, you cannot and should not trust the person to avoid hurting you in the same way again, because they see nothing wrong with what they did in the first place.

I'll get more into trust in a minute.

The second reason forgiveness is not evidenced by reconciliation is that sometimes the person who offended you has since gone away. Obviously in this case, you cannot reconcile with someone who is no longer around – nor can you return to how you were before. Does this mean you didn't forgive them? Of course not.

The third reason is that sometimes the offense is mutual, and while you have truly forgiven your offender, they have not forgiven you. The lack of reconciliation in this circumstance does not nullify your forgiveness.

And finally, you can't un-learn wisdom, and you shouldn't! If you have learned through your hurt that a person is capable of injuring you, wisdom dictates that you assess the situation and determine whether there is a risk of that person injuring you again, particularly in the same way. In some cases, it is clear that the person you are forgiving is aware of the injury they caused, genuinely remorseful, and you know their character well enough to determine whether their promises to be more careful in the future are sincere or plausible. If they are, perhaps reconciliation is possible, **but it is a separate act from forgiveness**.

However, often, in being hurt by an individual, it is the first time you have learned something new about that person. If it is not the first time, you need to wake up and learn something about that person. **They are capable of hurting you, and they may not deserve the same degree of vulnerability that you previously extended to them.**

It's kind of like a video game. If my husband is playing a video game, like Nintendo's *Pikmin*, for instance, there are different little armies he can take with him that have different strengths - some are fire-proof, some are water-proof, etc. Likewise, the "bosses," or big enemies, usually have a specific strength or weapon, such as fire or water, etc. If my husband goes to fight a new boss and realizes when he gets there that the boss breathes fire, and that boss proceeds to wipe out the army of water-specialized Pikmin he brought with him, when he comes back the next time to try again, he is not going to bring any water Pikmin with him. In so doing, he sets a boundary to protect his army.

In similar form, if you learn that a certain friend or acquaintance is comfortable lying to you, wisdom would dictate that you would not enter in to future interactions with that person expecting them to be honest. That is not unforgiveness. That is wisdom.

Some people may be able to earn back your trust, in which case reconciliation may be an option – but it has little to do with forgiveness.

Forgiveness is not trust.

Trust needs to be earned. Forgiveness needs to be given regardless of the circumstance, because it is for the good of the forgiver.

For Christians, the reason for this goes deeper. You are forgiven by the God of the Universe, even though you don't deserve it; so you should also forgive. Check out Matthew 18:21-35[4] in the Bible- if you need an illustration from The Man Himself to drive that point home.

What I learned in therapy about what forgiveness is *not* is that **I am not unforgiving just because I choose to distance myself from someone who can't stop taking advantage of or hurting me**. I am just not a masochist.

But what if that person undergoes a miraculous and thorough transformation to become a better person and has totally learned their lesson?!?

This is a really, really important question so please read my answer carefully: I will be happy for them, because the rest of their relationships will be better for the rest of their lives. But I am not obligated to put myself at risk again by reconciling.

So what forgiveness is not?

Forgiveness is not reconciliation

Forgiveness is not trust

Forgiveness is not masochism

Forgiveness is NOT an obligation to let them prove that they've changed

Forgive for your sake. Forgive for their sake. Pray for the ones who hurt you. Be kind. But practice wisdom. **Don't confuse sacrificial love with foolish self-harm.**

So how do you know if you've forgiven them?

You've sincerely let go of the offense. It no longer belongs to you. You will probably have to re-forgive someone for a long-lasting hurt over and over and over again. This doesn't mean you didn't *really* forgive them the last time.

For instance, say I was a victim of a horrible assault that left me with chronic pain. The physical injury is not going to be healed by my forgiving my assailant. There will be times, possibly every morning when I wake up in pain, possibly even multiple times a day, when I will have to re-forgive the injurer, because pain sucks and is frustrating. But the damage the attack did on my soul? That *will* heal over time as a direct result of my forgiveness. I may never lose the physical pain, but I don't have to harbor anger, bitterness, cynicism, fear, or distrust forever*. Some hurts keep hurting, and that hurt can beget anger. But give it up. Lay it down. Recognize that you are the one most harmed by your unforgiveness.

*If you suffer from injury, pain, or illness that is not the result of a person, this process is good even if the one you are angry with is God. It is not wrong to experience frustration with unfair or unexplainable afflictions, and such times still call for forgiveness, since it is *for the forgiver.*

63

1. Can you think of a time when you were hesitant to forgive someone because you felt it would return the state of the relationship to exactly the state it was before?

   _____

   _____

2. Flip back to this section at the end of Chapter 8 and look over your answers. How does this clarified definition of what forgiveness is *not* shift your perspective of the relationships you pondered in that section?

   _____

   _____

   _____

   - When you think of your fears surrounding forgiveness, are any of them alleviated when you realize that you can forgive them without

     - Reconciling?

     - Trusting them again?

     - Opening yourself up to more hurt?

     - Feeling obligated to let them prove they've changed?

- Think very carefully about the people you struggle to forgive in this new light. Journal it out! If you can forgive them without exposing vulnerability to the same afflictions, might you be better able to do it?

3. When you are ready to forgive, here is a handy little simple guide to forgiveness, **F.A.L.L.**:

    - **F** - Find the hurt. (The exercises in Chapter 8 can help you with this)

    - **A** - Acknowledge it. Understand it isn't your own failure or weakness that makes you vulnerable to hurt. You're *human*. And you can't treat an injury you won't acknowledge. That's the biggest risk of Leprosy and diabetes- numbing to a point of not noticing an injury before it's grown and become infected.

    - **L** - Lay it down. Literally visualize bundling up the anger, hurt, etc. and setting it down. If you believe in God, imagine you are laying it at His feet and trusting Him to take care of it.

    - **L** - Leave it there. Let go! Don't take it with you. This is where writing it out can be very therapeutic, and if visualization or having an action is helpful, you can even write the hurt down and dispose of it through any of several creative ways.

- You can write out in your journal the people or hurts you need to forgive and follow each with F.A.L.L. and work through them one at a time. Here is an example:

  - F - *I am hurt because [former best friend] forgot my birthday, and it still hurts even though they apologized.*

  - A - *This hurt me a lot because I made a big deal of her birthday, and birthdays are important to me.*

  - L - *I lay down my hurt and anger towards [former best friend] regarding my birthday.*

  - L - *I will move on with my life and [do _____ differently] to protect myself from similar hurts in the future, not out of bitterness, but out of self-care.*

4. Don't forget! You may need to forgive a specific hurt or person multiple times! This is not a failure on your part, it is just natural byproduct of a long healing process.

10

When Helping Becomes Stealing

When I started going to counseling, I wanted to work on figuring out what I could do differently about my friendships. I had realized I was feeling stressed out and bogged down with several relationships that were draining, not mutually fulfilling. I didn't know what I was doing to attract these friends, or how I could change my behavior within the relationships to prevent their falling into a habit of leaning too hard on me.

Can you relate at all?

My counselor asked me to describe these relationships. I gave a few descriptions in Chapter 6, but I'll briefly expand. I had some friends who didn't have many other friends.

Now, I've been raised to believe that a person doesn't need a lot of friends, they just need a few really good friends. **This is true if those relationships are**

healthy; if each party is, for the most part, putting in what they are taking out. But when a person desires many friends but doesn't have them, and/or expects the attention of several friends to be provided by one friend because that friend happens to be the only one they've got, that is not healthy or reasonable. It will make the one friend feel overwhelmed, drained, even resentful after a while.

The friends I am talking about were incredibly lonely people. Some had been repeatedly abandoned or abused by previous "friends" and were hurt, guarded, jaded. They told stories of bullies and mean girls and jerks, who started as friends and turned like Mr. Hyde into terrible people for no reason. Having had a couple of experiences with people who had behaved like this, I took their stories at face value without much question. Sure, there are two sides to every story, but it *wasn't very helpful* to be suspicious of a new potential friend, and it was clear that the story they told was at least totally true to *them*.

If they were wrong, I could **help** them by encouraging growth and maturity in my friendship with them, providing patience and honest feedback whenever they made me want to act like their previous friends, rather than abandoning them.

More and more, I noted as I reflected on these friendships that my experiences compounded on each other because, in some exceptional cases, this approach actually worked really well. It is sometimes kind and fair to give people an opportunity to *know* what they did wrong so that they can *understand* and adjust. A

68

few times in these moments of honest feedback, my friends thanked me for telling them and not just dropping them like so many people had, and they displayed a genuine change in behavior or attitude. This feedback looked something like this:

"You've talked in the past about people calling you annoying, and you felt it was unfair because they weren't specific about *how* you were annoying, and they didn't give you a chance to be better. So I want to tell you that I'm not going anywhere, but you calling me twice a day and texting me in between is really making me feel crowded, and I can understand people's inclination to pull away altogether because it's really intense. Can you please cut back on calling me to give me a chance to want to call you for a change?"

In several cases they seemed happy for the help, and showed a demonstrable change in behavior. But in as many cases, that person either made no change or made a brief change, only to settle back into old habits as soon as they felt safe that I would stick around.

I also noticed that in many cases, **the friend was content to make these changes in my friendship with them and not bother to make any new friends unless I introduced them.** Through this system of allowing me to bring them friends on a silver platter, at times it resulted in them overtaking my life. They were included in everything I did, with everyone I liked. A few took liberty to invite themselves along to *literally* everything I did because they knew I wouldn't say No, or because we now had mutual acquaintances involved. I then got feedback from some of the mutual acquaintances that the friend I'd introduced to the group had become annoying, clingy, etc, and that **they felt like they couldn't include me without including that friend, too.**

So Helping becomes Stealing in two contexts, one obvious, one not.

First, Helping can steal from you. **Helping is good, but only you can know how much is too much to give of yourself.** If you give too much to one person, *you* may become the bitter and jaded one when you feel spent. It may make you feel unwilling to make new friends because you are afraid of them leaving you wrung out like the last one did.

In the cases mentioned above, helping began to steal my independence and my understanding of boundaries - **I am not obligated to remain friends with someone** *even if they are willing to try to change for the better.* As I mentioned in the last chapter, if they change for the better and I do not choose to reconcile with them, the rest of their relationships and the rest of their life will still be better for that change. If they only change for my sake, it wasn't a true change anyway. Regardless, **reconciliation is my** *prerogative*, **not my obligation.**

But what my counselor pointed out to me was that helping can at times steal from the person you're trying to help. If I *help* the person standing right outside a conversation looking like they would like to join by pushing apart my friends to create a space, beckoning that person in, and asking them for their take on the conversation, **I may be** *stealing* **that person's opportunity to learn and develop their own social abilities.**

If I "*help*" my friend believe that there are people in this world who are truly loyal and will never leave, **I am** *stealing* **the life lesson that if you treat people terribly, they will not want to be around you.**

If I *help* a toddler put on his shoes every day, I am *stealing* his ability to independently learn how to put his shoes on, and **I am** *stealing* **his ability to apply that knowledge when I am not there.**

If I *help* a person make friends by taking it upon myself to take them along with me to all my own social events and introduce them to all my own friends, **I am** *stealing* **their ability to figure out how to make friends without** *my* **help.**

And if I *help* a person by introducing them to my friends and bringing them along to everything, **I am also** *stealing* **the option from my friends to decide whether they want to spend time with that person.**

I am *stealing* **the option from my friends to decide for themselves whether they want to have different boundaries than myself.**

I am *stealing* **from myself the option to have an identity separate from the friend I think I am helping.**

It is not the case that every time a person helps someone they are actually stealing, not by a long shot. But it is important to understand that sometimes helping steals a person's opportunity to grow. And in understanding this, we can all look more carefully at situations where we feel compelled to "help" and decide whether we are indeed being helpful.*

---

*My counselor helped me begin to learn the difference by assigning me to read the book *When Helping Hurts* by Steve Corbett & Brian Fikkert[5]. The book itself is mostly directed toward more global, large-scale attempts at helping and the more delicate sociological impacts they can have, but there is some amazing stuff in there that helps on a more personal level if you look for it.

Practice Your Art

1. Below are listed several scenarios. Write on the first line what opportunity the "helper" might be stealing. Write on the second line how the "helper" might *equip* the opportunity, or whether they might do best to step back and let the person learn on their own.

- A 20-year-old wrecks his car while texting at the wheel. His parents give him a stern lecture, replace the car, and continue paying the now higher insurance premium. After all, he needs to get himself to school.

   _____

   _____

- A school has a policy that allows students as many opportunities to re-take a test as many times as they need to pass it.

   _____

   _____

- A healthy 25-year-old is working part time & taking classes part time. Her parents cover her tuition and do not charge her for rent, groceries, insurance, or car repairs.

   _____

   _____

- A man works hourly, where employees are required to give notice 3 days in advance of the weekly schedule's posting for special scheduling and time off requests. The man's coworker repeatedly begs him to swap shifts with him because of social events, even at times with only hours' notice. The man often says yes, even at the detriment of his own plans, because he does not want to be "that guy".

- A man works front desk at a small office, answering phones, scheduling appointments, and making copies. His coworker is frazzled one day and asks him if he will type up her notes for a client and input some numbers into a spreadsheet for her. He says yes, and before he knows it, he is creating project budgets and she is dropping her notes on his desk for transcription every day without even asking. He does not protest because he did agree to do it for her once, and he does manage to make the time to get it done.

- A woman agrees to feed her next-door neighbor's pets while she is away on an unexpected overnight trip. Next thing she knows, she is taking care of the pets for weeks at a time, several times a year. But it's right next door, and the pets are familiar with her now. That's what neighbors are for, right?

- A man's mother-in-law often babysits his daughter, and buys her a treat every time she takes her to the grocery store. The man finds his daughter has come to expect to get a treat *every* time she is taken to the store, period. The man cannot afford to treat his daughter every time, but she throws exhausting tantrums whenever he tells her no. Now he has started budgeting to buy a small treat for his daughter each time they go to the store to keep the peace.

- A nutritionist is nominated by a friend to serve on the refreshments committee in the PTA without being asked first. He hears about it after he has been voted in to the position. He does not have the time, energy, or interest to serve in this way, but everyone is excited that he will be serving, he is the best qualified, and his friend says she will be embarrassed

for nominating him if he steps down, so
he takes the position.

_____

_____

2. Did you find yourself disagreeing that any or all
    of these are a "stealing" scenario?

_____

3. This is a time for you to get in touch with your
    motivations, your boundaries, and be honest
    with yourself. These examples were
    crowdsourced, and are snapshots of very
    common, classic enabling behavior. This
    interaction may be shedding light on why you
    were drawn to read this book in the first place!
    You can also use a journal to allow yourself to
    further explore your approach to relationships.

    •   Did seeing any of these scenarios on this
        list make you feel defensive?

    _____

    •   Why do you think you felt this way?

    _____

    •   Did seeing any of these scenarios remind
        you of someone?

    _____

    •   Recommend this book to them!

- Can you think of any examples from your own life that could have been on this list?

  - Write a few of them down on a separate paper or in your journal with space underneath each example.

  - Write the opportunities that may be stolen by "helping".

  - Write what behavior on the part of the helper might encourage those opportunities, rather than steal them.

  - What makes you nervous about the thought of *not* stealing, but encouraging opportunities in these ways?

_____

_____

_____

_____

_____

_____

_____

_____

_____

11

Sometimes People Are Friendless Because They're Crappy Friends

Having read this far, you know by now that I have had some rude, thoughtless, inconsiderate, or selfish friends in my time. You may wonder how I have allowed myself to *be* in friendships with people like that - isn't it my choice, in my control?

I found myself asking the same questions to my counselor. She had me describe how I had come to be friends with the specific people we discussed. The common thread among these friends was that they were often lonely when I met them, wounded by the hurt they had incurred from previous friendships, and hungry to be accepted by someone who wouldn't hurt them again.

It should be no surprise that one of my longest-running favorite songs is "All the Lonely People" by the Beatles.

But then my counselor pointed out - **they had all hurt me**. That's the whole reason I was talking about them in therapy. And, while "hurting people hurt people" is a *reason* that was easy for me to assign for their hurtful behavior towards me, I was learning that reasons aren't excuses (see Chapter 6). Then my counselor said something really brilliant and really blunt.

"Has it ever occurred to you that *sometimes* people are friendless because they're terrible friends?"

Definitely one of those AHA! moments in therapy that they teach us about in counseling classes. I had been gaining speed in my defenses and explanations and frustration and was stopped cold by this question.

We went on to process what it might mean if this were true. I truly always thought people are only lonely because of the failure of *others* to connect with them. *Surely* **it is society-at-large's fault that there are lonely people-** we learn from cultural phenomena like bullying and popularity that anyone left out must have been victimized by others' selfishness, meanness, or judgmentalness.

As someone who was bullied a lot early in my life, and as someone who always struggled to fit in and ultimately gave up altogether on the idea, this is a hard idea to swallow. My own experiences, and many I have witnessed, are proof to me that **it is not ALWAYS the**

79

case that someone has *earned* their feelings of loneliness or alienation.

In light of this, it was and continues to be a real struggle to me to grasp that, like everything else in the world, loneliness is not a black-and-white matter.

There are still people in the world who unfairly experience loneliness at the hand of others, purely because of their meanness, selfishness, judgmentalness. But as it turns out, **there are also people who experience loneliness because of their own actions**, the way *they* treat their friends, or people who aren't yet friends and now never will be.

There are *also* people, I suspect the majority of people, who are lonely because of a very messy combination of these two scenarios. They are truly and unjustly alienated because they said or wore something deemed unacceptable, then they decide perhaps they need to call the shots in their next friendships, and become aloof or cynical or critical. Or they are so wounded by their hurts that they begin to cling WAY TOO HARD to those who are kind to them, making the burden of their happiness someone else's responsibility. Then they get rejected for their unfriendly behavior, and are hurt by this rejection, and a cycle begins.

My counselor challenged me to *continue being empathetic*, but to take a step back and give myself an opportunity to be a little more impartial when I see someone lonely who "just needs someone to be kind to them."

I realized I can have a little bit of a martyr/savior/contrarian attitude trifecta when it comes to the human condition. I want to *PROVE* every kind of cynicism wrong and single-handedly spearhead a trend of acceptance and unconditional love, one outcast at a time!

This is, to be honest, still totally my philosophy - though perhaps not the single-handedly part. But **I thought that it was my job as a follower of Jesus Christ to *love* people into healthier lives.**

This friend is used to being abandoned and lashes out and hurts me so I won't hurt him first? I'll love him *harder* every time he hurts me so he will realize he is loveable and that *someone* won't abandon him.

That friend who is a constant gossip who makes me wonder what she says about me to others? I'll patiently look for positive things to say about the people she gossips about, teach her by example to be loving.

This huge group of mega-churchgoers overtly leaving someone awkward out of the conversation? I'll invite them in, invite them along, and force that group to act out the love of Christ - **that's what'll cure sin!**

Oh.

Didn't sound so bad until that last bit, did it?

While I strive constantly to be *like Christ*, I am NOT the Almighty. And **what I have really been trying to do is heal people on behalf of Jesus, *all by myself.***

81

And shockingly, that hasn't been working out so hot for me – or for them.

> *"Not by might*
> *nor by power,*
> *but by my Spirit"*
> *says the Lord.*
>
> *Zechariah 4:6*

As a Christian I need to trust God and lean harder on Him for wisdom and discernment about who to love and how to love them.

I also need to back off on my martyr attitude that it's ok if they hurt me as long as they come out of it a fraction better. I lose my efficacy in the relationships God *wants* to use me in when I spend so much of myself fighting against people who don't know how not to hurt me.

Sometimes people are lonely because they're crappy friends. Those people may never learn their lesson, but I actually provide them a crutch when I insist on sticking around through their crappy behavior.

If a child hits his playmates, but their parents insist that they include him anyway, and circumvent the natural consequences of his actions, how will he ever learn to stop hitting?

And how will his peers ever learn to discern healthy interactions from unhealthy ones?

With children, as in this example, it is important to facilitate consequences for the child who is hitting that are reasonable for their age and maturity level, and have a conversation with both the child and their playmates about how to treat one another, and the natural consequences of being violent or unkind. With adults, a parallel situation should reflect the difference in the maturity of the offender, and the consequences may require fewer "teachable moments."

Another thought: surely *OUR* version of the times when we've been wronged is the most accurate, *right*? We came out of it hurt, therefore they *must* have been the crappy friend? When I feel alienated, I am learning to reflect and really try to impartially consider whether I was in the wrong. It is certainly not the case all the time, but it happens more than I am comfortable admitting. I *know* I have been a crappy friend before. I have found I am particularly bad at reacting to someone else's wrongdoing with my own wrong. I can still learn from such cases, even if reconciliation isn't in the cards. **We build upon the story of our character with every interaction.** Bowing out with grace and integrity even when we have been wronged is an essential cornerstone of who we are becoming as we mature.

Practice Your Art

1. Be honest with yourself. Do you have a bit of a hero complex in your approach to some or all of your relationships?

   _____

   _____

   - Do you have any friends who are functional, happy the majority of the time, and to whom you are one of several healthy friendships?

     _____

     _____

   - Do you have any friends who do not *need* you for something?

     _____

     _____

   - Do you actually like being around those friends, or does it make you feel uncomfortable, like you don't have a purpose around them, or they may not actually want you around?

     _____

     _____

- Do you feel fulfilled exclusively in meeting others' needs?

  - This is not to suggest that you should not feel fulfilled when you meet people's needs. But do you have any other means by which to feel fulfillment and purpose?

    _____

    _____

    _____

- Are you able to befriend people who do not need to be rescued, or cared for?

    _____

2. What benefits are there to having at least some mutually beneficial, low drama, give-and-take, balanced relationships? This may seem like an obvious question, but indulge me and list them below. Sometimes things that seem obvious don't get enough attention.

_____

_____

_____

_____

_____

_____

_____

_____

_____

- Was this list more difficult to come up with than you expected?

  - If so, why do you think that is? Sometimes we literally do not know what is good for us, at least not off the top of our heads. That translates to what mistreatment we are willing to put up with.

---

3. Are you guilty of being a relationship martyr?

- Do you willingly return to a situation you know will hurt you either emotionally or physically because you have hope that your perseverance will result in a positive change in the other person?

- Consider Chapter 10; what opportunities might your "help" be stealing from that person?

---

4. If you are lonely, I know it is hard, but consider any feedback you have gotten from those friends you feel abandoned you:

- Could you have been a better friend?

_____

_____

- Don't sacrifice your "muchness" (those elements of your personality that make you unique), but have you sacrificed social courtesy?

  - Personal space?

  - Reasonable boundaries?

  - Basic consideration?

- Even if you can't or aren't interested in reconciliation, take every opportunity you can to learn from all your relationships how you may be able to improve yourself and your approach to your other relationships.

12

The Art of Saying No

So how do we distinguish what to do with lonely people? Above all, know your motives. **Know when you are filling what void for whom.** If you want a friend, and you are looking for someone to be in a two-way relationship with you, enter into the friendship with whomever you find understanding **what you need**, **what you expect**, and **what they need**, and **what they expect**. It is no more a friendship if only *your* needs are being met than it is if only *theirs* are. If you see a person who tugs at your heartstrings, who you just want to help, enter into that relationship only if you have the energy, time, & emotional equity to spare without it being returned in kind.

Imagine your time, energy, and emotional equity are all stored as liquid in a big pitcher that is ideally meant to be *FULL*. It is your job as a matter of self-preservation to become and remain constantly aware of the status of that pitcher. Learn to check in with yourself. If your "pitcher" is barely ¼ full, you need to know that you'll be empty if you pour into someone. If you look at your current circumstances and can identify someone pouring into you, or some activity that refills you - if you feel like you're overflowing! - now is a great time to invest in someone. But take care to pour out at a sustainable pace. Know when to back off a bit if you lose a source that had been filling you up, or when a person you're pouring into is demanding more from you. And know when you're in a place of balance and bask in it!

Identify relationships that give you as much as you invest, and a few relationships or activities that help fill you up, and a few relationships or activities that you pour into.

The art of saying No is understanding your limits *before* **you are already waist-deep,** entering into every interaction with those protective limits and boundaries informing the choices you make and actions you take.

Practice Your Art

1. Imagine yourself as a water pitcher.

    - How full are you?

    _____

    - How empty?

    _____

    - How consistently are you at that level?

    _____

    - Do you wish your level were higher?

    _____

2. Make a list of the things, people, and activities in your life (including family) that pour into your pitcher:

    _____
    _____
    _____
    _____
    _____

3. Make a list of the things, people, and activities in your life (including family) that you pour into:

    _____
    _____
    _____

4. Look at the two previous lists.

- What things, people, and activities made it on to both lists?

_____

_____

_____

- Is one list longer than the other?

_____

  ▪ Does that reflect the state of your pitcher?

  _____

  ▪ If not, why not? Is there one person or thing that is giving or taking a large amount proportionate to everything and everyone else?

  _____

  _____

5. Is there anyone who is pouring significantly more into you than you are pouring into their life?

_____

- Some people put more in than the other for a season of a relationship. This is not a bad thing - it's part of the gig. But think carefully. If they have been pouring more into you than you have into them for more than a season, consider whether it is time for you to give back. What is keeping you from pouring back into them?

- It is common for people to only be able to think of a limited number of ways they might pour in to their relationships and loved ones. We tend to think of our own needs and desires, and not be aware of alternatives. It is possible, in some cases, to actually pour more into them than you are pouring out of yourself! Or even, in the most symbiotic relationships, be more filled up yourself in the process of filling them. (Someone may love to come up with new recipes, another person may have a special dietary restriction. Both can be filled up by a relationship in this case.) So think creatively about how you may be able to pour in to those who have been pouring in to you for a season, especially longer. Even a simple but sincere Thank You can go a really long way. List your ideas.

_____

_____

_____

6. Is there anyone or anything that you are pouring significantly more into than they are?

_____

- Is it simply a season, or a constant state of the relationship?

_____

- If it is a constant state, it is time to start identifying when you need to say No. Take this opportunity to write some ideas. (Note: Even if it is a legal dependent, who you have no choice but to care for, if your relationship with a person is *that* off-balance, you need to take a step back, consult a counselor, life coach, or trusted friend, and find solutions to alleviate your output. It may mean hiring or enlisting outside help to care for that person. It may simply mean intentionally looking for ways they try to pour back in to you and taking a moment to appreciate them in your exhaustion.)

_____

_____

_____

_____

_____
_____
_____
_____

7. In case it isn't clear, any relationship in which at
    least one party is *consistently* pouring out
    significantly more than they are getting back is
    a codependent one. Write your thoughts as you
    consider this in light of the previous questions.

_____
_____
_____
_____
_____
_____
_____
_____
_____
_____
_____
_____
_____

13

Cracking the Code:
What Lies at the Heart of Enabling

Up to this point, you may have begun to wonder when we are going to get to the reason you started reading this book - how and when should we say "No"? I hope it is becoming clear, however, that you don't simply start with No. There are a lot of steps of growth and self-reflection before that backbone becomes strong. At about this point in my journey, I was thinking about a hoarder I had worked with, and found myself trying to explain to a friend of mine the complex psychology and family dynamics that contribute to how a person becomes a hoarder. As I navigated my own knowledge of the experiences of hoarders I had worked with, and in turn several addicts, and in turn several codependents, I had an epiphany.

What all these demographics have in common is what I talked about at the very beginning of this book. They are all extreme examples of a common issue of codependency and enablement. They also all have a common root.

My epiphany was as follows: At the root of people pleasing, or enablement, is the belief on the part of both enabler and enabled that **Love is measured by how loved the receiver feels.**

Let me say that again.

The root of codependence is the belief that love is measured by how loved the receiver feels.

Think about it. Time and time again, we are all inclined to measure the world by this ruler.

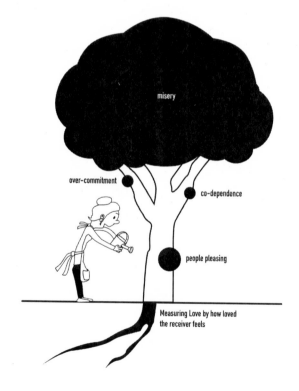

misery

over-commitment

co-dependence

people pleasing

Measuring Love by how loved
the receiver feels

I had a client who was freshly recovering from drug addiction who was seeing me to work on deep anger and unforgiveness she had for her family because they would not take her into their home. How could they *abandon* her in a homeless shelter (one that provided NA meetings, interim jobs, classes, free counseling, free clothing, 3 meals a day, relatively safe sleeping accommodations, showers, mentors, career aid, legal aid, and free medical services) when they had an empty room in their house? She sincerely felt they did not love her, they did not care about her.

I also have a loved one who has struggled with drug addiction, who probably went through the exact same questions in the exact same circumstances, and as I worked with this client, I knew from experience with *my* addict that I loved them so deeply, and that in the moments when I had to say no and they felt the least loved by me, I had done it out of the deepest love for them, and healthy boundaries to protect myself.

In the case of my hoarding clients, they felt compulsively attached to their collections. Every item represented hope for putting it to use, comfort, or the love of the person it reminded them of. They therefore reacted to their family members attempting to remove those items as an act of malice. It felt to the hoarders like an attack that either incidentally or intentionally hurt them, and literally stole from them.

Meanwhile, their families were looking at the big picture; they saw skyscrapers of boxes piled to the ceiling around their loved one's bed, waiting to fall on them as they slept. They saw stacks upon stacks of paper piled next to stocks of aerosol chemicals, blocking the only exit in the event of a fire. They saw expired food waiting to make their hoarders sick, and ultimately an overall reflection in physical space of the depression and overwhelmed state of mind their loved ones were dealing with inside their heads.

They wanted to clear the hoard not to steal away the hoarder's hope for future projects, but to restore the space in which projects might actually be done. They were not wanting to remove the comfort and security provided by the objects the hoarder collected, but to introduce *real* security, safety, and the comfort of a clean, useable home. Finally, they were not intending to undermine the love that the hoarder associated with sentimental objects, rather they desired to create room in their loved one's life to experience relationships in the present, and create new memories.

I have also had times when I have *felt* abandoned, unloved by God. I was angry at Him, or felt betrayed by Him. How could He let me suffer in these ways? Why wouldn't He give me the deepest desire of my heart?

How often have you come across, whether in your own life or in talking to others, people who are bitterly angry with God because they did not feel loved by Him? How many times in the Bible did this happen?[6]

But God is sovereign. God is loving. We are dumb. Our comprehension of love is finite. In the same way a 2-year-old may not understand WHYYY her daddy won't let her touch the pretty red coil on the stove, *doesn't he want her to be happy???*, we do not always know how to measure His love.

So how *do* we measure love?

Practice Your Art

1. What do you think of this idea of a new measure of love?

   _____

   _____

   _____

2. Can you think of a time when you have done something out of love for someone and they did not feel loved by the act?

   _____

   _____

   _____

3. Can you think of a time when someone has told you they were doing something out of love and you did not feel loved?

   _____

   _____

   _____

4. Below are listed several scenarios. Circle the option that would be most likely to *feel* like love to the recipient:

   - A 5-year-old wants to stay up and watch TV with his father on a school night:

     - His dad turns on a movie and plunks the child onto the couch beside him.

- His dad insists he complete a bedtime routine and get into bed at the usual time.

- A 14-year-old wants her parents to buy her a ticket to attend a concert with a friend unsupervised:

  - Her parents offer to give her opportunities to earn her ticket and attend the concert with her.

  - Her parents buy the ticket, drop her off, and tell her to have a good time.

- A 16-year-old named Tim calls his friend and asks him to cover for him while he stays the night with his girlfriend, and tell Tim's parents he was at the friend's house when they ask:

  - His friend tells Tim he is sorry but he won't lie for him.

  - His friend says ok and lies for Tim.

- A 23-year-old named Jayce moves in with a friend after his parents kick him out. He promises to pay half the rent as soon as he can get on his feet. He lines up interviews occasionally, but remains unemployed after 5 months.

- Jayce's friend continues to pay the bills and nags Jayce, finding job postings for him and loaning him interview clothes.

- Jayce's friend sets a firm deadline by which time Jayce needs to pay rent or find somewhere else to go.

• Meg is getting ready to go on a special date to celebrate her wedding anniversary. Her best friend calls her crying and tells her she's had a fight with her new boyfriend, and begs Meg to meet up for dinner and talk it out.

- Meg calls the restaurant to cancel her dinner reservation, figuring she and her husband can get a bite to eat after the show, and squeezes a meeting with her friend in before her now-postponed date.

- Meg tells her friend she has plans, but offers to talk on the phone while she finishes getting ready.

• Ray's mother moves into the house across the street and develops a habit of showing up uninvited, visiting several times a week, and staying for hours at a time. She insists that in retirement, Ray and his children are her only joy in life.

- Ray gives his mother a key to his house and encourages his wife to be grateful for the free babysitting.

- Ray gently insists that his mother call before coming over, and encourages her to look for other sources of joy to add to her life.

14

Just Because It Hurts
Doesn't Mean It's Not Healthy

Once it starts to sink in that love is not measured by how loved the receiver feels, a lot of shifts start to happen in your world view. One big shift is realizing that **just because something hurts, doesn't mean it isn't healthy**. I learned this in several applications, some of which are quite personal, but the lesson itself I believe is essential for everyone.

I once worked as a chef on a Dude Ranch in Colorado. We had over 60 horses, and a staff of experienced wranglers who took care of them. I remember one time a horse had been spooked and kicked up, landing slightly on a fence post and badly lacerating his leg. Every day, one of the wranglers would have to scrub out the wound, eliminating any dead or infected tissue and washing away the bacteria. I watched the process a few times, and as I'm sure you can imagine, the horse did *not* care for the treatment. It was a large wound, about the size of my hand, deep, and clearly incredibly painful. But if the wrangler had not taken the time to tend to it, the wound would have certainly become a massive infection, and the horse would not have survived without his care.

It is very difficult to find yourself in a position where you have to inflict pain (emotional or physical) on someone for a greater good. This whole book has touched on a recurring theme that I have had trouble with boundaries. To put it simply, I had to learn that **just because someone might be hurt by my withdrawing from their life, or setting boundaries, doesn't mean it's not a healthy thing for me to do.**

Think of it this way. Say a couple has a young son with severe autism. One of his consistent behaviors is that he loves to run into the street. When his mom and dad restrain him from his impulse to run into the street, he kicks and screams and *genuinely, truly* believes his parents hate him, don't love him, because he does not understand why they're keeping him from doing what he *needs* to do. At *any* point will this boy's parents decide perhaps they should let him run into the street every now and then so that *for once* he'll believe that they love him? (Note: This is an imagined, hypothetical scenario, so I'm taking the liberty to narrow out all other symptoms, scenarios, alternative opportunities for his parents to express their love for their boy.) If his parents really love him, won't they let him do what he really wants? Or if his parents *REALLY* love him, will they keep him from harm's way, even though he doesn't understand - will NEVER understand - that they do it out of love, and they don't *want* to hurt his feelings?

I don't care if my kid hates me every day of the rest of my life, and is *genuinely, truly* convinced I am ruining his life, I am not going to let him run into traffic to convince him otherwise.

If my adult child calls me a traitor, hates me, and believes I don't love her because I won't financially support her by letting her live under my roof with a severe drug addiction, I'm not going to enable her to convince her otherwise.

Sometimes people's perceptions of our feelings towards them are just wrong.

In fact, usually, the more unhealthy a person is, the more incorrect their perceptions of how we treat them, how we feel about them. **It doesn't help for us to affirm their delusion by displaying whatever behavior they *think* expresses love to them.** That is not the same thing as "speaking someone's love language*". It is not an issue of language or communication if a person has a harmful misconception of what it means to actually be loved. Incorrect perceptions in this context are not merely

---

*You may have heard of a popular book series by Gary Chapman centered around the concept of *The Five Love Languages*. *The Five Love Languages* books are intended to help strengthen healthy relationships and bring people closer together through better understanding how they give and receive healthy love, and how their partner gives and receives healthy love. Its focus on "languages" is about the various levels at which individuals communicate with one another, and aiding in translation for people who may not understand their relationship partner's language.

about the *method* of delivering love, but what is actually delivered.

A simple example is if a person is taught from childhood that the name for a piece of brightly colored hard candy on a paper stick is "apple," when they ask their friend for an apple, and they are given a piece of fruit, they will not think their need has been met. That is not a translation error. They are both speaking English. The first person just does not know what an apple is, and is unaware that they do not know what an apple is. And if they ask for an apple, because they have heard that apples are good for them, and they are given lollipops, they won't think anything is wrong but they will not receive the health benefits of an apple.

Only at least in the story of apples and lollipops, only the recipient is harmed in the confusion. With love, a receiver's wrong definition almost always harms the giver, too.

In counseling I realized that many times when I have failed to set a healthy boundary, I have failed to do so because the person I was setting the boundary with pushed back, indicated that my boundary hurt their feelings, or otherwise deprived them of something they felt they had an inalienable right to. I might succeed at setting the boundary only to have them test it, giving me guilt trips, crying, or misinterpreting it to mutual friends or family if I enforced it.

The really hard thing about it is, much of the time I really felt that the person genuinely didn't understand that I didn't want to hurt them, I needed the boundary for myself. It isn't as if they were always just whining or manipulating or overreacting to get their way - **they truly believed the only reason I was enforcing my boundaries was to hurt their feelings.**

But just because they don't understand why it's healthy, or that it's healthy, doesn't mean it's not healthy.

I've learned that **just because my boundaries cause someone emotional distress, doesn't mean I am wrong in setting them.**

In fact, it isn't just my own emotional health that boundaries like these are promoting.

If a person is deeply, genuinely, truly hurt by my setting a healthy boundary, it is possible *they* have a problem with boundaries. Read that again. *They* may have an unreasonable emotional connection or dependence on their friends or family.

(It *is* possible, by the way, for family to be codependent on family. You are not exempt from the need to set boundaries with your family, just because you are often emotionally closer to them than friends.)

And it's not my obligation, even as a counselor/coach by trade, to fix or heal or help them with the problems that led to them being hurt by my boundary.

Practice Your Art

1. Check in with yourself. How do you feel as you read and process this chapter?

_____

_____

_____

2. Can you think of any examples of when something might both hurt and be healthy?

_____

_____

_____

3. Have you ever had to do something, such as discipline a child, where you were doing something out of love, but they did not understand?

_____

_____

_____

4. What scenarios or relationships (if any) in your own life came to mind as you read this chapter?

_____

_____

_____

_____

5. Thinking about the themes in this chapter, have you gained any new insights on difficult-to-accept boundaries that your loved ones may have set with you at some point?

_____

_____

_____

6. What concerns or fears do you have as you think about how this chapter might apply to your own life?

_____

_____

_____

_____

7. What relief or validation are you experiencing as you think about how this chapter might apply to your own life?

_____

_____

_____

_____

_____

15

Adjusting to a New Ruler:
When God is Saying No

I got married at age 26.

Most people probably consider that a pretty reasonable, appropriate age to get married. I admit, though, for several years I would have thought it about 3-4 years too late.

I wasn't exceptionally impatient about finding a husband, or getting married, but **I had an expectation that it was inevitable**. You see, I have a healthy, strong body, wide hips, and a strong, long-term desire to have *lots* of kids. So obviously, God *made* me to be a mother - it only makes sense that He'd give those kids a dad.

This wasn't, of course, the only reason I wanted to get married - not by a long shot - but it was the source of my certainty that I *would* get married. God wouldn't want to waste such excellent mothering material.

Then about 2 years before I met the man to whom I am now married, around age 24, I had an epiphany of contentment. I came to this realization through a combination of two things. First, God was speaking to me through the letters of Paul in the Bible. Second, I was getting super annoyed with some of my friends.

See, I had several friends who had the exact same mentality as I had. The desire of their heart was to have a husband, or to have children, so *obviously* that was what God had in mind for them.

Why would God give us a deep, burning desire for something if He wasn't intending to give it to us? That certainly doesn't *feel* loving.

But I noticed that as we moved away from college graduation age, some of my friends had... slowed their lives to a crawl. They didn't put any serious thought into what they might be doing in 5 or 10 years if they didn't get married, because such a scenario would be unacceptable - *preposterous*! A few of them were a bit older than me, and were getting impatient and frustrated because **they felt the time when they had to be independently responsible for their lives, without the benefit of partners to share their burdens with, should have passed by now**.

I found myself getting annoyed with their attitudes, their sense of entitlement about marriage, and their naïve assumption that they were *owed* husbands because they *wanted* them. I saw it as irresponsible, unwise to put oneself in a position where focus on something that is not a guarantee blocks out consideration of the alternatives. I also saw it as dangerous, making them vulnerable to settle for *someone* because the idol of marriage was more important than being alone longer in order to wait for someone *right*.

And then I realized I was acting the same way. I was just as certain and confident that eventually, probably soon, I would meet someone. After all, if I want to have 5-7 kids and not have minors in my house at retirement age, I had better get started soon! I wasn't being as verbal about it as some of the people in my circle, but I absolutely assumed it was something I was guaranteed. **The only difference between myself and those friends was time.** The time between when I had expected to meet my husband and this revelation was brief, so I wasn't quite impatient yet. I had only just entered my unexpected "waiting period" until wifehood.

God started speaking to me through 1 Corinthians 7:7-9

> " I wish that all of you were as I am. But each of you has your own gift from God; one has this gift, another has that. Now to the unmarried and the widows I say: It is good for them to stay unmarried, as I do. But if they cannot control themselves, they should marry, for it is better to marry than to burn with passion.[7]"

I realized, much to my chagrin, that I actually felt I could control myself. I didn't consider celibacy an impossible thing, and while I was a normal, healthy 24-year-old with normal, healthy drives, "passion" was not a major force in my desire to be married. **I realized that it might possibly be God's plan for me to remain single.**

The implications of this for my life were staggering. I realized how much of my attitude was centered around my assumption that soon enough, everything in my life would change, and I would be able to factor in another person to make decisions about my future, handle money, and glorify God through the raising of a cluster of little Christians from scratch.

I had to determine what about my life needed to change if I decided then and there never to marry. **What about my behavior and career and goals would be different if I stopped factoring in the possibility of a husband?**

That was when I realized I had already begun to mentally settle into the meantime. I stopped. I made my own choices about my career based on what I could actually see myself doing forever to actually support myself. I dared to dream about and get excited about the prospect of being single and having the freedom to change my course at will, enjoy solitude, be undistracted in the pursuit of my faith, and minister to other singles.

I still dated, sure - I wasn't against marriage if it happened. But it **no longer defined my life as a single**

person as a waiting room for the next stage of life. Single adulthood *was* a stage of life - possibly my last. A unique, fun, liberating, awesome stage that allowed me to be in a one-on-one relationship with my true Beloved, God.

When I pushed past that assumption that God's love should be measured by my fulfilled expectations, I began to learn a new, better peace. I experienced a deeper and more trusting relationship with Him.

Fast forward a few years. I met my husband under incredibly... serendipitous circumstances. It has been evident from the first moment I saw him that God truly brought us together, saved us for each other, prepared us for one another. We got married.

My husband and I were on the same page about having a big family from the beginning. I won't get too deep into specifics here, but we took a non-approach to birth control from the beginning of our marriage. We felt if God really wanted to give us a baby, He would, whether we tried to stop Him or not.

Additionally I will own that at almost 27 years old, I was already a little impatient to start having kids - if I had married at 23, I could have had like 3 kids by now!

And so began my new meantime. How wasteful was I? To become so wrapped up in the next "promised" (definitely never promised) stage of motherhood that **I viewed my time alone with my brand new, AMAZING husband as a consolation prize** until I got pregnant?

I was anxious and frustrated, and impatient for several reasons. I was desperate to prove to myself and to the world that everything was healthy here - no problems getting pregnant! After all, the implications of infertility would throw a wrench in my only plan for married life. Then I caught myself.

How in the world could I have learned so little from my time as a single adult? **Hadn't I learned better than to only plan the future around people who hadn't arrived yet and** *had no guarantee of ever coming?*

Why did I have such a sense of entitlement about pregnancy, anyway? Just because my body is healthy, I'm automatically *owed* an opportunity to use it? Just because I had the organs for sex didn't mean I was *owed* an opportunity to use them, either!

The truth is, once I was willing to acknowledge it, that we are not promised anything, I felt free; true contentment.

Once I was willing to lay down my personal idea of what God's love looked like, He taught me a much better love than I could have fathomed.

Jesus was celibate. He didn't have any children of his own. He LOVED kids. But that wasn't what God had in mind for his ministry. The Apostle Paul, as far as we know, was single, and he additionally had a "thorn in [his] side". He never indicated that he felt entitled not to feel pain but he never let it get in the way of his ministry. In fact, his pain has since ministered to so many others who read of his faith in the face of that pain when they are coping with their own. And I know Paul had a deep, permeating *desire* not to be in pain.

It turns out, sometimes God allows us to have desire so that we may learn from being deprived.

It turns out, desire and want can serve a different function in God's purpose than telling us what we're entitled to.

I still have a deep, burning passion for motherhood. I have a specific desire to experience pregnancy that is difficult to put into words. And I am still young - I know this. Four years is really not *that* long to be trying unsuccessfully to get pregnant in the grand scheme of things. **I have not given up *hope*, but it's about time I give up the meantime.**

The stage I am in could be the last stage I am ever in. And what a beautiful stage it is! How utterly, unbelievably wasteful for me to treat it like it's just a waiting room for me to impatiently focus on what lies beyond.

My husband and I are open to other options, too - adoption and foster care are on our minds. But even these are not simple or guaranteed. I have learned, and been scolded by my younger, single, content self, that **to covet, even that which is good, is to be entitled and ungrateful**.

Practice Your Art

1. What stage of life are you in right now?

_____

_____

2. Do you covet the "next" or a "previous" stage, or even a missed one?

_____

_____

_____

3. What, if anything, do you feel you are "missing" in your current stage?

_____

_____

_____

_____

_____

4. What blessings of your current situation might you be ignoring in your belief that you are "owed" whatever it is you are "missing"?

_____

_____

_____

_____

_____

_____

_____

_____

5. What opportunities do you have in this stage that you wouldn't or won't have in any other?

_____

_____

_____

_____

- Are you taking advantage of them?

_____

- If not, *why not*?

_____

_____

_____

_____

6. (If applicable) how are you using your own expectations as a ruler to measure God's love?

_____

_____

_____

_____

_____

(This Chapter is primarily for Single readers, feel free to skip to the next chapter if it doesn't apply to you.)

16

On Matters of Romance: Codependence and Tarzan

Imagine Tarzan, swinging through the trees from one vine to the next; grabbing hold of the next vine before letting go of the last one. This is the mental picture I get whenever I hear friends of mine start telling me about their newest love interest only days or weeks after their last breakup. I imagine them afraid to let go of one crush or relationship without already having their grasp on the next one, never wanting to let their feet touch the solid, stable ground of being totally unattached. I've nicknamed this behavior "Tarzaning," and it seems to be an epidemic in western culture, particularly among young adults. We can't stand to be alone, particularly after a breakup. I think it's because there is a fear deep down that if we let our feet touch the ground, we may never get back up into the trees again! This is dangerous and short-sighted logic.

What does Tarzaning look like in real life? If any or all of the following apply:

- A person who has not been single for longer than 2 months since they started dating, or in a very long time (say, 2-3 years or longer)

- A person who already has their next interest picked out before their previous relationship actually ends

- A person who actually feels ill-at-ease, anxious, frustrated if they find themselves single

- A person who actually feels ill-at-ease, anxious, frustrated if they find themselves not only single, but without anyone to daydream about

- A person who may not have the talent for actually getting *into* relationships, but also can't seem to think about anything other than doing just that. That is to say, even some people who *have* been single, even for a while, can be Tarzaning if they are forever and without any breaks *trying* to get into a relationship.

- A single person who is always talking to or flirting with 2 *or more* people at a time so that they have backups just in case one doesn't work out. This behavior in itself isn't necessarily "bad", but if it describes *you,* ask yourself what are your motives *behind* it - is it simply that you're free and single and enjoying it and not quite settled on one person yet, or that you have a few people interested and you're waiting to get to know them better? These are reasonably healthy reasons. *But*

- if it is because you find yourself totally averse to the thought of having NOBODY to flirt with, NOBODY to be interested in, and heaven forbid NOBODY interested in you,

- if when you're honest with yourself you realize your self-worth would be significantly injured if you found yourself for any extended amount of time without anybody interested in you. These are signs that you have an unhealthy attachment to the **idea** of a relationship.

This is the main point: it is not healthy for you or your relationships if the primary reason you are in them is that you can't stand the thought of being single. It's not fair to your partner if they are just the placeholder that allows you to keep the security blanket of being in a relationship. It is not fair to you *or* your partner to be/enter/remain in a relationship if you know somewhere, deep down, that it is the companionship you are attracted to as much as or more than the person you are with.

DON'T let the fear of being alone allow you to stay stuck in a sub-par relationship!!!!

I'm willing to bet you know someone or *are* someone with Tarzaning habits. If you're not sure, check out the

Application section at the end of this chapter, and please, be honest with yourself.

So, you know what Tarzaning looks like, and I've vaguely alluded to it's being a dangerous pattern of behavior, but what are the real negative consequences to Tarzaning?

- You aren't giving yourself opportunity to recover. There are huge benefits to taking time post-relationship to reflect and grow, allow the hurt to sink in, and get practice coping, recovering, and moving forward on your own, without the aid of distraction. I understand (no, REALLY, I understand) that everything about this sounds uncomfortable and preferably avoided, but it's like taking your medicine, or going to physical therapy - it takes a little pain to become stronger, more flexible, even less sensitive in some cases.

- I'm going to revisit the concept of reflection. You need time and space between love interests to look at yourself, reflect on the previous relationship, and consider what you could have done differently, or what went wrong, or what early signs you can look for in the future to indicate problems before they have to happen all over again.

- You aren't allowing yourself to get enough distance from the relationship that you can be honest about the person you were with: is there a pattern in your failed relationships? Do you tend to go for emotionally unavailable partners?

123

or perhaps overly attached and needy ones? It is going to be difficult, if not impossible, to really be honest with yourself about these missed red flags if you already have someone else on the hook who displays the same traits.

- You aren't allowing yourself time and opportunity to grow as an individual. If you are constantly in a relationship, without time in between, you probably aren't allowing yourself enough time for yourself, for independent hobbies, interests, friends...

- If you are religious, your relationship with God may suffer. If you are fixated on being with another person, your thoughts and prayers can become fixated on that relationship. This is normal, but until you have found that one person and married them, you should be continuing to focus on your walk with God individually. Your time as an unmarried person is a special time, so special that Paul recommends it as a preferable choice over being married, if one can stand to make the choice, as he says in 1 Corinthians 7:32-35:

> "I would like you to be free from concern. An unmarried man is concerned about the Lord's affairs—how he can please the Lord. But a married man is concerned about the affairs of this world—how he can please his wife— and his interests are divided.

An unmarried woman or virgin is concerned about the Lord's affairs: Her aim is to be devoted to the Lord in both body and spirit. But a married woman is concerned about the affairs of this world—how she can please her husband. I am saying this for your own good, not to restrict you, but that you may live in a right way in undivided devotion to the Lord.[8]"

- It is possible there are things deep in your heart and mind that you are avoiding through the distraction of relationships. If you are compelled to avoid being "alone" for too long, you probably need more than anything to do just that. If you become anxious at the thought of being single, and remaining that way, it is time for you to try it out and tackle the thing you are so afraid of.

So now that you've identified the problem, and perhaps you're beginning to recognize the consequences of this Tarzaning behavior in your own life, what can you do to address it?

- First of all, let's start with a baby step - if you are in a relationship, take a week apart from your shmoopy little snugglewhiskers. See how you react to being apart for a few days. You may actually show symptoms of anxiety, or find you don't know what to do with yourself. You may come to realize that you've lost touch with a lot of your friends since you've been moving from one relationship to the next. You may also remember some of those independent interests and hobbies that you haven't thought to touch since you started dating - pick up that paintbrush, read a book! This isn't intended to break you up, necessarily, but it will help you move towards placing less weight on companionship, which is healthier for the relationship in the long run.

- If you are currently between relationships, or find yourself approaching that possibility, make a deal with yourself, just as an experiment: if you really think there's no problem here, you can stand to be single for 3-6 months. You can still spend time with the opposite sex, but take advantage of that time to get to know them!

- If you find yourself worried that they will move on to someone else if you aren't available to be with them the moment they ask, frankly that logic is ridiculous. If this person is worthwhile, and finds YOU worthwhile, they will be able to stand waiting and getting to know you for a few months, and the relationship will be stronger for it!

- Here is where I start to touch on a raw spot, though, because we may be uncovering your real reason for Tarzaning: you may realize, through this experiment, that you are insecure, that you don't believe yourself that you are worth waiting for. You ARE. If your interest is not willing to wait for you, that means NOTHING about your own worth: It says everything for that person missing an amazing opportunity, or finding someone better fitted for them. You need to start assuming and telling yourself that if a person isn't ready for you when you are ready for them, or vice versa, it is not the right time, if ever there is one, for that relationship. If you force it, it will probably end or be riddled with problems, but if you embrace God's perfect timing, and trust him to bring you the right people at the right time, you'll find yourself happy regardless of your relationship status.

- ABOVE ALL, immerse yourself in good works, and prayer if you are religious. Get outside yourself a little, work on strengthening your relationship with God and serving those around you. These things will reward you whether you are single or an old married person; these practices are more certain to place quality people in your path than anything else you can do with your time.

Practice Your Art

1. When was the last time you were single for longer than a month?

   _____

2. What did you initially like about the person you're currently with?

   _____

   • Was it just their apparent attraction to you?

   _____

   • What about the last person?

   _____

3. Is it possible you date whomever is convenient and interested rather than allowing yourself opportunity to be discerning and really get to know the person?

   _____

4. Are you willing and able to:

   • Wait until you know the next person well enough to be sure they're actually a good match for you?

   _____

- Remain single however long it takes until someone really quality comes along, instead of settling for whoever is there?

_____

5. *Are you settling for fear of being alone?*

_____

6. Do you believe you are worth waiting for?

_____

- If not, why not?

_____

_____

_____

17

How Do I Change
the Relationships I Have for the Better?

You should have begun to recognize by now that the key to journeying out of codependence, people-pleasing, and over-commitment is in healing relationships and setting good boundaries. You may be wondering where to begin implementing change in your life? I hope that you can look back over the time you have spent reading this book and already note the beginnings of subtle and progressive shifts in your thoughts and behaviors in a healthy direction. However, it is a lot to take in - where do you start? What steps can you take?

Here is a sort of refresher of what you've been learning that doubles as a diagnostic you can run for any relationship whose state of health is unclear to you, or for which you are unsure what exactly is wrong. This can help you to identify underlying causes for the stress in your life and/or your relationships.

- Are you doing this "act of love", this "Yes," out of habit?

  - Is it just routine that you do this for that person or organization?

- Are you breaking promises you've made to yourself when you say Yes to "loving" someone else?

  - I'm not saying be selfish, but if you're reading this book, odds are the promises you make to yourself are few, far between, and extremely important for your mental, spiritual, emotional, and/or physical health. **Love is not neglect of self**.

- Are you actually preoccupied with *loving*, or are you preoccupied with *not disappointing*?

  - Is it an act of genuinely considering the best interest of the receiver of your love, or are you acting because you are compelled, to avoid feeling bad for saying no?

If you are religious, measure against your relationship with God - Is your relationship with each person reducing the efficacy of your relationship with God?

- Is it drawing you away from God?

- Or is it BOOSTING it, pushing you closer to God?

  - Think a little extra about this one. Just because a relationship puts you in proximity to the church, or even ministerial events, doesn't mean it's boosting your relationship with God. As a people-pleaser-in-recovery, I can tell you that sometimes saying Yes and committing to a church activity can pull you further from God. Measure your love for others, for your ministry, for the church by its encouragement of your walk with God, not distraction from it.

- When you are hurt or wronged by the other in a relationship, do you measure forgiveness by how close to your previous "normal" you can get?

  - Are you measuring forgiveness by reconciliation, your ability to trust the person in the same way as before they hurt you, or *whether they feel forgiven*?

  - Or are you measuring it by your own progress in healing from the hurt, increase in wisdom, and perhaps even your ability to better protect yourself from repeat inflictions of the same kind?

132

- Look hard at your acts of love; are you *purely* helping or are you stealing someone else's opportunity to learn, to step up, or to have that void filled by God?

- Are you most strongly motivated in your relationships by the desire to prevent the other from hurting?

  - When you think in terms of what is best for the other long-term, for their greater health (mental, physical, emotional, spiritual), wholeness, and *autonomy*, is your approach to loving them pushing them towards that?

- Reflect: are you in the relationship or saying Yes to the organization to fill a need in yourself?

  - A need to be needed, a need to feel appreciated, a need to fix someone?

    - Your love for someone else isn't measured by how well your own needs are fulfilled by them.

  - Are you depriving yourself of the opportunity to let God or others fill that need?

- Measure other relationships - is your involvement here reducing your efficacy in other relationships?

  - Is it reducing efficacy in your ministry, career, pursuit of health (mental, physical, emotional, spiritual), wholeness, or autonomy?

18

A New Measure of Love

So if the root of codependence is the belief that love is measured by how loved the receiver feels, how *do* we measure love? How can we know how to love others well if not by whether they *feel* loved? I have put together a sort of handy go-to referral list you can skip to when you find yourself feeling overwhelmed, over-committed, or in the midst of a possibly unhealthy relationship. Think of it as a **Relationship Ruler.**

I am aware not everyone reading this book is a Christian. By now, it is glaringly obvious that I am, and I draw much of my philosophical context from scripture. However, it has been observed by many scholars of all backgrounds throughout the ages that the Christian bible is an excellent resource for philosophical study and life wisdom, even if you merely regard it as classical literature. I therefore urge you to see this checklist for the wisdom it provides and the light it can shed on your relationships, regardless of your degree of interest in the source.

The bible talks a lot about the Fruits of the Spirit. I've found great inspiration from them in my search for a new way to measure love. They're basically a measure of the best parts of God as they show themselves in our lives. Galatians 5:22-23a lists the Fruits of the Holy Spirit, "But the fruit of the Spirit is love, joy, peace, patience, kindness, goodness, faithfulness, gentleness, and self-control..." Jesus said in Matthew 7:17-18, "Likewise, every good tree bears good fruit, but a bad tree bears bad fruit. A good tree cannot bear bad fruit, and a bad tree cannot bear good fruit." And again in Matthew 12:33, "Make a tree good and its fruit will be good, or make a tree bad and its fruit will be bad, for a tree is recognized by its fruit.[9]"

Here is your super simple ruler for measuring love in your life: Look at your fruit. Is it Good or Bad?

Is your love bearing good fruit? Check in by taking a step back from the relationships in your life and considering:

- Is this relationship cultivating Love in my life and the life of the other?

- Is it cultivating Joyfulness in my life and the life of the other?

- Is it producing more Peace than strife?

- Am I learning Patience*?

> *Not every relationship is 100% happy, but are the interactions with the other in the relationship helping me or the other learn patience? Or am I becoming less and less tolerant, finding my fuse with that individual getting shorter?

- Am I being Kind to the other? Are they being Kind to me?

What Goodness is this relationship producing?

- Is this relationship driving me deeper into my Faith, or further from it?

- Are we each able to be Gentle with one another?

- Am I able to have Self-Control in this relationship?

  - Does this person or this relationship cause me to feel out of control, or to do things I have resolved not to do?

  - Does this relationship cause me to lose my temper, to gossip, or to be harmful to myself or others, or compromise my integrity?

Now that you have "measured" the love in your relationship, consider what, if anything, about that relationship needs to change. If your relationship is producing "bad" fruit such as anger, strife, gossip, abuse, joylessness, selfishness, etc., where is that coming from? Could it be a misunderstanding of how best to love each other? Are you exchanging mislabeled lollipops when you both need apples?

Ultimately the formula for how to love is simple, at least in concept - the application is a lifelong learning endeavor! It goes like this:

If your action of love produces Good Fruit, it is real, healthy love.

If your action of love produces Bad Fruit, or does not produce any good fruit, it needs to be evaluated. Consider how applying the Art of No to your life may begin to shift the quality of the fruit you are producing. It will be difficult for you to assess the quality of your fruit if you have not familiarized yourself with what good fruit actually *looks* like.

Now go and love well.

Appendix

Chapter 3: **I Am as Responsible to Keep Promises to Myself as to Others**

[1]***Scope Creep*:**
"Definition - What does Scope Creep mean?
Scope creep refers to a project that has seen its original goals expand while it's in progress. As the term suggests, scope creep is a subtle process that starts with small adjustments and ends up resulting in projects that take far longer to complete or even fail before they are finished. Even if the project is completed, scope creep can result in final deliverables that look nothing like what was originally envisioned.

"...Scope creep can occur for a number of reasons, including:
A poor understanding of the original project
Changing market conditions
Competing forces within a company
To avoid the worst kinds of scope creep, a project manager should consider even minor adjustments to the original project scope carefully and rework time lines, provide new estimates and communicate with the stakeholders before integrating changes. This should filter out all but the most important concerns."

"What Is Scope Creep? - Definition from Techopedia." Techopedia.com, www.techopedia.com/definition/24779/scope-creep.

Chapter 5: **God's Calling Vs. The Approval Of Others**

[2]"From that time Jesus began to show his disciples that he must go to Jerusalem and suffer many things from the elders and chief priests and scribes, and be killed, and on the third day be raised. And Peter took him aside and began to rebuke him, saying, "Far be it from you, Lord! This shall never happen to you." But he turned and said to Peter, 'Get behind me, Satan! You are a hindrance to me. For you are not setting your mind on the things of God, but on the things of man.'" (Matthew 16:21-23)

"BibleGateway." *Matthew 16:21-23 NIV - - Bible Gateway*, www.biblegateway.com/passage/?search=Matthew 16:21-23&version=NIV.

[3]"In Damascus there was a disciple named Ananias. The Lord called to him in a vision, "Ananias!"
"Yes, Lord," he answered.
The Lord told him, "Go to the house of Judas on Straight Street and ask for a man from Tarsus named Saul, for he is praying. In a vision he has seen a man named Ananias come and place his hands on him to restore his sight."
"Lord," Ananias answered, "I have heard many reports about this man and all the harm he has done to your holy people in Jerusalem. And he has come here with authority from the chief priests to arrest all who call on your name."

141

But the Lord said to Ananias, "Go! This man is my chosen instrument to proclaim my name to the Gentiles and their kings and to the people of Israel. I will show him how much he must suffer for my name."

Then Ananias went to the house and entered it. Placing his hands on Saul, he said, "Brother Saul, the Lord— Jesus, who appeared to you on the road as you were coming here—has sent me so that you may see again and be filled with the Holy Spirit." Immediately, something like scales fell from Saul's eyes, and he could see again. He got up and was baptized, and after taking some food, he regained his strength."

"BibleGateway." *Acts 9:10-19 NIV - - Bible Gateway*, https://www.biblegateway.com/passage/?search=Acts+9%3A10-19&version=NIV.

Chapter 9: **What Forgiveness Is NOT**

[4]"Then Peter came to Jesus and asked, 'Lord, how many times shall I forgive my brother or sister who sins against me? Up to seven times?'

Jesus answered, 'I tell you, not seven times, but seventy-seven times.

'Therefore, the kingdom of heaven is like a king who wanted to settle accounts with his servants. As he began the settlement, a man who owed him ten thousand bags of gold was brought to him. Since he was not able to pay, the master ordered that he and his wife and his children and all that he had be sold to repay the debt.

'At this the servant fell on his knees before him. 'Be patient with me,' he begged, 'and I will pay back everything.' The servant's master took pity on him, canceled the debt and let him go.

'But when that servant went out, he found one of his fellow servants who owed him a hundred silver coins. He grabbed him and began to choke him. 'Pay back what you owe me!' he demanded.

'His fellow servant fell to his knees and begged him, 'Be patient with me, and I will pay it back.'

'But he refused. Instead, he went off and had the man thrown into prison until he could pay the debt. When the other servants saw what had happened, they were outraged and went and told their master everything that had happened.

'Then the master called the servant in. 'You wicked servant,' he said, 'I canceled all that debt of yours because you begged me to. Shouldn't you have had mercy on your fellow servant just as I had on you?' In anger his master handed him over to the jailers to be tortured, until he should pay back all he owed.

'This is how my heavenly Father will treat each of you unless you forgive your brother or sister from your heart.'"

"BibleGateway." Matthew 18:21-35 NIV - - Bible Gateway, www.biblegateway.com/passage/?search=Matthew 18:21-35&version=NIV.

Chapter 10: **When Helping Becomes Stealing**

[5]Corbett, Steve, et al. *When Helping Hurts How to Alleviate Poverty Without Hurting the Poor ... and Yourself.* Moody Publishers, 2014.

Chapter 13: Cracking the Code: What Lies at the Heart of Enabling

[6]*Psalm 77:1-9*:
"I cried out to God for help;
I cried out to God to hear me.
When I was in distress, I sought the Lord;
at night I stretched out untiring hands,
and I would not be comforted.
I remembered you, God, and I groaned;
I meditated, and my spirit grew faint.
You kept my eyes from closing;
I was too troubled to speak.
I thought about the former days,
the years of long ago;
I remembered my songs in the night.
My heart meditated and my spirit asked:
'Will the Lord reject forever?
Will He never show his favor again?
Has His unfailing love vanished forever?
Has His promise failed for all time? Has God forgotten to be merciful?
Has He in anger withheld his compassion?'"

Psalm 44:9-26:

"But now you have rejected and humbled us;
you no longer go out with our armies.
You made us retreat before the enemy,
and our adversaries have plundered us.
You gave us up to be devoured like sheep
and have scattered us among the nations.
You sold your people for a pittance,
gaining nothing from their sale.
You have made us a reproach to our neighbors,
the scorn and derision of those around us.
You have made us a byword among the nations;
the peoples shake their heads at us.
I live in disgrace all day long,
and my face is covered with shame
at the taunts of those who reproach and revile me,
Because of the enemy, who is bent on revenge.
All this came upon us,
though we had not forgotten you;
we had not been false to your covenant.
Our hearts had not turned back;
our feet had not strayed from your path.
But you crushed us and made us a haunt for jackals;
you covered us over with deep darkness.
If we had forgotten the name of our God
or spread out our hands to a foreign god,
would not God have discovered it,
since He knows the secrets of the heart?
Yet for your sake we face death all day long;
we are considered as sheep to be slaughtered.
Awake, Lord! Why do you sleep?
Rouse yourself! Do not reject us forever.
Why do you hide your face
and forget our misery and oppression?
We are brought down to the dust;

our bodies cling to the ground.
Rise up and help us;
rescue us because of your unfailing love."

Ruth 1:13b, 19-21:
"No, my daughters. It is more bitter for me than for
you, because the Lord's hand has turned against me!"

"So the two women went on until they came to
Bethlehem. When they arrived in Bethlehem, the whole
town was stirred because of them, and the women
exclaimed, 'can this be Naomi?'
'Don't call me Naomi,' she told them. 'Call me Mara,
because the Almighty has made my life very bitter. I
went away full, but the Lord has brought me back
empty. Why call me Naomi? The Lord has afflicted me;
the Almighty has brought misfortune upon me.'"
*Note: Naomi means *pleasant*, Mara means *bitter*

Jonah 4:1-9:
"But to Jonah this seemed very wrong, and he became
angry. He prayed to the Lord, 'Isn't this what I said,
Lord, when I was still at home? That is what I tried to
forestall by fleeing to Tarshish. I knew that you are a
gracious and compassionate God, slow to anger and
abounding in love, a God who relents from sending
calamity. Now, Lord, take away my life, for it is better
for me to die than to live.'

But the Lord replied, 'Is it right for you to be angry?'

Jonah had gone out and sat down at a place east of the
city. There he made himself a shelter, sat in its shade
and waited to see what would happen to the city. Then

146

the Lord God provided a leafy plant and made it grow up over Jonah to give shade for his head to ease his discomfort, and Jonah was very happy about the plant. But at dawn the next day God provided a worm, which chewed the plant so that it withered. When the sun rose, God provided a scorching east wind, and the sun blazed on Jonah's head so that he grew faint. He wanted to die, and said, 'It would be better for me to die than to live.'

But God said to Jonah, 'Is it right for you to be angry about the plant?'

'It is,' he said. 'And I'm so angry I wish I were dead.'"

Bible passages taken from NIV - Bible Gateway, www.biblegateway.com

Chapter 15: **Adjusting to a New Ruler: When God is Saying No**

[7]"BibleGateway." *1 Corinthians 7:7-9 NIV - - Bible Gateway*, www.biblegateway.com/passage/?search=1 corinthians 7:7-9&version=NIV.

Chapter 16: **On Matters of Romance: Codependence and Tarzan**

[8]"BibleGateway." 1 Corinthians 7:32-35 NIV – *Bible Gateway* www.biblegateway.com/passage/?search=1 Corinthians+7:32-35&version=NIV

[9] Bible passages taken from NIV - Bible Gateway, www.biblegateway.com